MYANMAR'S FOREIGN POLICY
Domestic influences and international implications

JÜRGEN HAACKE

ADELPHI PAPER 381

Routledge
Taylor & Francis Group

LONDON AND NEW YORK

First published June 2006 by Oxford University Press for the
International Institute for Strategic Studies, Arundel House, 13-15 Arundel Street,
Temple Place, London, WC2R 3DX

This reprint published by Routledge
2 Park Square, Milton Park, Abingdon, Oxon, OX14 4RN
For The International Institute for Strategic Studies
Arundel House, 13-15 Arundel Street, Temple Place, London, WC2R 3DX
www.iiss.org

Simultaneously published in the USA and Canada
by Routledge
270 Madison Ave, New York, NY 10016

Routledge is an imprint of the Taylor & Francis Group

Transferred to Digital Printing 2008

Director John Chipman
Editor Tim Huxley

British Library Cataloguing in Publication data
A catalogue record for this book is available from the British Library

Library of Congress Cataloguing in Publication data

ISBN 0-415-40726-5
ISSN 0567-932X

Publisher's Note
The publisher has gone to great lengths to ensure the quality of this reprint
but points out that some imperfections in the original may be apparent.

Contents

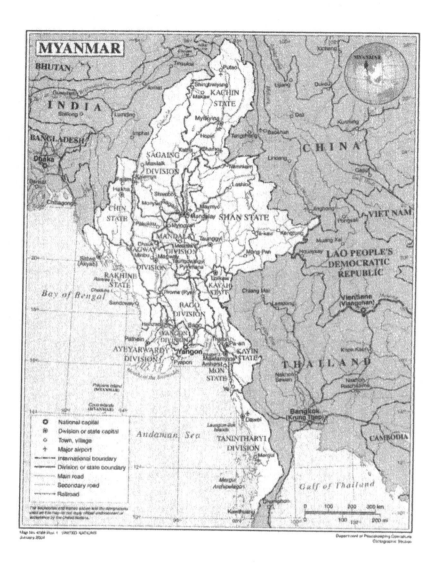

Map produced by the UN Cartographic Section and reprinted with the permission of the Secretary of the United Nations Publications Board.

GLOSSARY

AASROC	Asia–Africa Sub-Regional Organisation Conference
ADB	Asian Development Bank
AIPMC	ASEAN Interparliamentary Myanmar Caucus
AMM	ASEAN Ministerial Meeting
APEC	Asia Pacific Economic Cooperation
ARF	ASEAN Regional Forum
ASC	ASEAN Security Community
ASEAN	Association of Southeast Asian Nations
ASEM	Asia–Europe Meeting
ASSK	Daw Aung San Suu Kyi
BIMST-EC	Bangladesh, India, Myanmar, Sri Lanka, Thailand-Economic Cooperation
CPB	Communist Party of Burma
CLMV	Cambodia, Laos, Myanmar, Vietnam
ECHO	European Commission Humanitarian Aid Office
FDI	Foreign direct investment
FTA	Free Trade Area
GMS	Greater Mekong Sub-region
IAI	Initiative for ASEAN Integration
ICG	International Crisis Group
ICRC	International Committee of the Red Cross
IDSS	Institute of Defence and Strategic Studies, Nanyang Technological University, Singapore
IFI	International financial institutions
ILO	International Labour Organisation
ISEAS	Institute of Southeast Asian Studies
ISIS	Institute of Strategic and International Studies
KNU	Karen National Union
MI	Military Intelligence
MTA	Mong Tai Army
MOGE	Myanma Oil and Gas Enterprise
NC	National Convention
NCGUB	National Coalition Government of the Union of Burma
NGOs	Non-governmental organisations
NOEX	Nippon Oil Exploration (Myanmar)
NSCN	National Socialist Council of Nagaland
NLD	National League for Democracy
ODA	Official Development Assistance
PLA(N)	People's Liberation Army (Navy)
PMC	Post-Ministerial Conference
RTA	Royal Thai Army
SIGINT	Signals intelligence
SLORC	State Law and Order Restoration Council
SPDC	State Peace and Development Council
SSA	Shan State Army
SSNA	Shan State National Army
SURA	Shan United Revolutionary Army
UNCHR	United Nations Commission on Human Rights
UNGA	United Nations General Assembly
UNHCR	Office of the United Nations High Commissioner for Refugees
UNSC	United Nations Security Council
UNSG	United Nations Secretary-General
UWSA	United Wa State Army

INTRODUCTION

For the first time in the country's post-Cold War history, on 16 December 2005, the situation in Myanmar became the subject of a comprehensive briefing given by United Nations Under-Secretary-General for Political Affairs Ibrahim Gambari, during informal consultations of the UN Security Council (UNSC). The briefing was the outcome of months of intense lobbying by the administration of George W. Bush to address what Washington has called the 'deteriorating situation in Burma'. According to Washington, the military government is responsible for actions that not only make it an 'outpost of tyranny', but also that threaten international peace and security. As the US permanent representative to the UN argued, the ruling military regime's domestic practices have resulted in 'things like ethnic cleansing, refugee flows, international narcotics trafficking, trafficking in persons, [and the] failure to act adequately on threats like HIV/AIDS or avian flu'.[1] Only days earlier, Malaysian Foreign Minister Datuk Seri Syed Hamid Albar, then-chairman of the Standing Committee of the Association of Southeast Asian Nations (ASEAN), and Malaysian Prime Minister Abdullah Badawi, host of the 2005 ASEAN Summit, publicly reprimanded Myanmar in an unprecedented manner. While the US government sees the UNSC as having a critical role to play in promoting positive change in Myanmar, ASEAN countries have been keen to 'learn first-hand of the progress' in Yangon's implementation of its road map to democracy that was announced in late August 2003.[2]

These developments suggest new momentum in international and regional efforts to bring Myanmar to book for its widely perceived domestic failures, above all the continued detention under house arrest of Nobel Peace Prize laureate Daw Aung San Suu Kyi (ASSK), the lack of dialogue between the military government and the National League for Democracy (NLD), the rules and composition of the National Convention (NC), the widespread violation of human rights, especially in ethnic-minority areas, including the displacement of civilians and forced labour, the failure to stem the production and trafficking of narcotics and the deteriorating humanitarian situation.[3] They have also raised impor-tant questions, as to whether the United States – much criticised for its penchant for unilateralism – might succeed in mustering support for a reinvigorated multilateral strategy towards Myanmar, whether ASEAN might be part of such a strategy, how Myanmar might respond and what implications these developments might have for the international poli-tics of Southeast and East Asia.

It is by no means assured that diplomatic efforts undertaken either by the United States or within Southeast Asia and the United Nations will achieve what critics of Myanmar's military regime are so eager to see happen. International pressure to date, including sanctions, has certainly impacted on the country's economy and international standing, but has remained politically ineffective insofar as the fiercely nationalistic State Peace and Development Council (SPDC) – which was known as the State Law and Order Restoration Council (SLORC) until 1997 – has chosen to defy the international community. Significantly, this defiance has been sustained and reinforced by a foreign policy that has taken advantage of the stake that neighbouring countries hold in Myanmar's development and stability and their desire to promote cooperation and regional integration. China, India and the ASEAN states have offered the military regime diplomatic protec-tion to varying degrees. How Myanmar will ultimately fare in the impending stage of the battle of wills between the military regime and its international detractors is in large part a question of how successful its foreign policy has already been and how effective it promises to be in the future.

This paper examines the objectives, means and effectiveness of Myanmar's foreign policy under the current military regime headed by the SPDC. It identifies the primary drivers and basic principles of Myanmar's foreign policy and the main goals that the SPDC has pursued *vis-à-vis* the country's immediate neighbours as exemplified by the state of its relations with China and India; the significance of the country's relationship with ASEAN; and the difficult nature of Myanmar's interactions with Japan, the West and the United Nations. Myanmar could, in Washington's view, be a test case on whether the US can build up support for and rely on a multilateral approach to bring 'freedom' to a country experiencing sustained domestic repression. It explores the likely consequences of increased political pressure on Myanmar's foreign policy, how the regime would seek to counteract or undercut this pressure and whether, in light of the likely response by Myanmar, Western policy-makers should further reflect on the available policy alternatives.

Main arguments

There are five core arguments that are crucial to the dissemination of Myanmar's foreign policy. The first is that it both serves and is constrained by what might be termed the military regime's perceived 'domestic political-security imperative'. Essentially, this imperative encapsulates the regime's main political and security objectives and the belief that these objectives must be secured if at all possible whatever the political and economic cost and whatever the objections of foreign governments. Two elements of the imperative stand out: national unity and sovereignty. For the current leadership this implies, firstly, continuing the military's state-building project and ending satisfactorily the decades-long civil war with ethnic minorities and, secondly, braving all attempts to replace prematurely the current military regime with a political successor characterised by the same weaknesses as past civilian governments. In practice, the military's perceived domestic political-security imperative has resulted in a multi-pronged approach to force ethnic insurgents to subscribe to the unitary state in which the military retains a major role. Equally, the imperative has obligated the military to fight off internal and external challenges to its rule and authority.

The second, related argument is that the regime's defence of the perceived domestic political-security imperative has come at a price the generals have indeed so far been willing to pay. Deprived of Western assistance, the country has remained mired in a state of economic transition from the failed policies of the 'Burmese Way to Socialism' to the imperfect embrace of a market economy, which is confronted by substantial development needs. Myanmar's quest for international standing has been undermined by its focus on the political-security imperative, as is evident in reactions to the junta's stubborn defence of its snail-paced seven-step roadmap to democracy. The defence of the political-security imperative against external challenges has even brought new threats to the country's sovereignty; US diplomacy to ensure that Myanmar comes and remains under UNSC scrutiny vividly illustrates this, but still the SPDC remains defiant.

Third, Myanmar's difficult relations with Western countries mask the substantial evolution of its foreign policy in the post-Cold War period, which has seen the new military rulers go beyond the neutralist and at times isolationist outlook adopted by General Ne Win's previous military regime. This evolution initially involved political and military alignment with China. Subsequently, the regime embraced a 'look-around' policy and, as opportunities presented themselves, opted to join sub-regional and regional institutions with neighbours from South Asia, Southeast Asia and East Asia. In consequence, Myanmar has managed to achieve a balance of sorts in its relations with all of its neighbours, thereby enhancing its diplomatic leverage, and is now firmly integrated into regional international society. Contrary to the opinions and expectations articulated in the 1990s, Myanmar has also avoided becoming a political client of China.

Fourth, although designated a pariah and scolded for its defiance of appeals and sanctions intended to foster political democracy and greater respect for human rights, above all from 2000–02, Myanmar's domestic politics and foreign policy shifted gear with a view to markedly improving relations with the wider international community. This move was encouraged by former prime minister General Khin Nyunt and linked to his preparedness to work towards breaking the political deadlock with the NLD and its general-secretary from an apparent position of strength. During the brief period over which this gear-change was sustained, cooperative relations with the UN in particular reached new heights. The period also saw non-state actors (for example, the International Committee of the Red Cross [ICRC]) finally granted permission to visit detainees and to investigate the situation of civilians affected by conflict along the Thai border;[4] Amnesty International was also allowed to visit Myanmar for the first time in early 2003.[5] In the event, however, political intransigence in the domestic theatre and the hard hand played by the West and Japan undermined this approach. With priorities unambiguously refocused on the imperative of domestic stability and regime security, the abrupt end to political reconciliation with ASSK has had major foreign-policy implications for Myanmar since 2003.

The fifth argument is that one of the major failings of Myanmar's foreign policy is the unwillingness or incapacity to recognise that continued and largely unmitigated defiance may not only prolong and deepen cycles of suspicion and hostility with regime critics in the West, but may also undermine those in Southeast Asia who have been broadly sympathetic. This failing in part reflects the seemingly ingrained inability for political accommodation and conflict settlement within Myanmar. Yet the attempts by Western states to coerce the military into political submission may lead to unintended and undesirable consequences. Western pressure on Myanmar has so far not caused the regime to abandon or de-emphasise the political-security imperative and it is difficult to see why this should change. Faced potentially with a serious challenge to its pursuit of the perceived political-security imperative, Myanmar's foremost leaders may conclude that they have to ensure against the possibility of the US making headway towards its stated objective of involving the UNSC in forcing the military's hand. The only external insurance ultimately available is a Chinese and/or Russian veto, although the likelihood of securing the former is possibly greater. This could still prompt the SPDC to develop significantly closer ties with China and leave it more vulnerable to future political demands. It is also possible that if ASEAN leaders were to push the military government too hard, Myanmar might reassess ASEAN's relevance, causing the regime to withdraw from active cooperation, or even consider leaving the Association. The first development would be undesirable for geopolitical reasons; the second would be potentially devastating for Southeast Asia because of the implications for the planned establishment of an inclusive ASEAN community. In other words, it is not only developments on the domestic front, as Yangon's critics usually maintain, but also the development of its foreign policy that have potentially major regional ramifications. Western policy-makers, moreover, need to consider whether the possibility or reality of any major realignment of Myanmar's foreign policy could lead to disagreement between Western powers and their friends and allies in Southeast and East Asia.

CHAPTER ONE

The Political-Security Imperative and Foreign Policy Goals

The *Tatmadaw* (armed forces) is Myanmar's premier institution and it has no serious institutional competitors.[1] Since 1988 it has ruled the country through the SLORC and its successor, the SPDC.[2] The SPDC is comprised of Myanmar's top military decision-makers.[3] Yet it has been left to the core military leadership in Yangon, now in Naypyidaw, to flesh out collective policy decisions outside infrequent SPDC meetings in ways similar to a standing committee, albeit informally. From 1992 to 2004, Myanmar's top three leaders were Senior General Than Shwe (SPDC Chairman), Vice-Senior General Maung Aye (SPDC Vice-Chairman) and Khin Nyunt (initially as Secretary-1 of the SPDC and head of Military Intelligence [MI] and, as of 2003, as prime minister). During his time as the regime's third in command, Khin Nyunt gained a reputation for being relatively sophisticated in his approach to international affairs. He assumed not only an increasingly important role in guiding Myanmar's diplomacy, but was also the principal architect and driver of Yangon's foreign policy towards the West and the wider international community between 2000 and 2003. However, following an apparent escalation of disagreements among the top leaders over the pace, success and sustainability of policies he initiated, as well as the role and practices of MI, and his refusal to abandon the post of chief of MI, General Khin Nyunt 'retired' in October 2004.[4] He was subsequently convicted on eight separate charges, including bribery, corruption and insubordination, and given a suspended prison sentence of 44 years in 2005. The distinction hitherto made between 'internationalists' and 'isolationists' among military rulers thus, at least temporarily, lost much of its usefulness.[5]

At present, the core leadership of the SPDC comprises Than Shwe, Maung Aye and the likely successor to the top post, SPDC member General Thura Shwe Mann. In contrast to Khin Nyunt, Thura Shwe Mann has been careful to stay in the background and to demonstrate proper respect to both his elders, not least in foreign policy matters, and has so far not developed any obvious foreign policy specialisation. The current Secretary-1, Lieutenant-General Thein Sein, and Prime Minister General Soe Win do not possess Khin Nyunt's previous influence. Although the principle and practice of collective leadership and consensus applies, the ultimate decision-making power continues to rest with the junta chairman, Than Shwe, who has retained the defence portfolio and thus remains a member of the cabinet. This affords him control over which issues will be decided by the cabinet and which will be taken up by core members of the SPDC. That said, by the late 1990s, 14 committees and organisations had been organised along the lines of a task force and were acting as 'supra-ministerial steering bodies cutting across ministerial portfolios'.[6] In relation to foreign-policy making, the Foreign Affairs (Policy) committee is the most significant cross-ministerial committee. Chaired by the prime minister, it meets on a weekly basis and puts policy recommendations forward to the cabinet. The foreign-minister is the committee's secretary. With this structure, the foreign-policy decision-making process is both top-down and bottom-up.

Until its emasculation in October 2004, the MI apparatus (under successive labels such as the Directorate of Defence Services Intelligence or the Office of the Chief of MI) played a substantial role in foreign policy formulation and implementation. The Office of Strategic Studies, formed in 1994, also took a 'strong interest in Burma's expanding international relations, in effect directing the diplomatic activities of the Foreign Ministry'.[7] For much of the time since the end of the Cold War, the foreign-affairs portfolio was managed by only two ministers: U Ohn Gyaw, a previous director general of the political department, and U Win Aung, a former ambassador to London and Bonn who also possessed considerable UN experience. Notably, while formally responsible to the minister, the influence of ambassadors has depended on whether they have benefited from direct access to the core military leadership. Since September 2004, the foreign minister has been U Nyan Win, who is an alumnus of India's National Defence College and a former vice-chief of Myanmar's Armed Forces Training. He is supported by two vice-ministers: U Kyaw Thu, son of former president Dr Maung Maung, who moved to the Ministry of Foreign Affairs in 1999 with a military background, and U Maung Myint, who was also appointed in September 2004 and is a former Light Infantry Division commander. U Nyan Win has reportedly established a strong reputation for seeking and taking advice from top career officials. However, in the initial stages of his tenure, which coincided with the ubiquitous politics of survival within the elite and the government bureaucracy in the wake of the Khin Nyunt's ouster, foreign policy-making ground almost to a halt.[8]

Declaratory and operational foreign policy

Myanmar's present regime remains committed to pursuing an 'independent and active foreign policy' first proclaimed by the Burma Socialist Programme Party under Ne Win in August 1981. Demonstrating continuity even with the 'independent' foreign policy of the 1970s and the policy of 'positive neutrality' pursued by Prime Minister U Nu, the military government claims that Myanmar is 'everybody's friend but nobody's ally' and that it still takes a 'just and independent' stand on international issues based on their relative merits and in line with national interests. A dedication to the Five Principles of Peaceful Coexistence has also been retained.[9] So has the principle that Myanmar will only accept foreign aid that is beneficial to national development and comes with no strings attached. However, its 'independent and active foreign policy' has been adapted to a changing environment. The country's declaratory foreign policy now emphasises: maintaining friendly relations with all nations and good relations with neighbouring countries in particular; the continued support of, and active participation in, the United Nations and its affiliated organisations; the pursuit of mutually beneficial bilateral and multilateral cooperation programmes; regional consultation and beneficial cooperation in regional economic and social affairs; and active participation in the maintenance of world peace and security as well as opposition to imperialism, colonialism, neo-colonialism, interference, aggression and domination of one state by another and the creation of equitable economic conditions.[10] Burma's post-independence foreign policy of non-alignment and independence was very much a reflection of the perceived external sources of threat, particularly in its immediate environment, as well as its difficult domestic conditions.

Influences on operational foreign policy

By committing Burma to neutralism or non-alignment in foreign policy, the civilian government under U Nu following independence in 1948 sought to evade becoming enmeshed in the Cold War big power confrontation. The violation of Burma's territorial integrity by US-supported Kuomintang troops in the early 1950s and the outbreak of the Korean War of 1950–53 reinforced this goal. While non-aligned, Burma remained particularly sensitive to the need to carefully manage relations with China. Beijing was a major security concern for Burma from the 1950s onwards, initially because of its revolutionary policies and a border controversy. The latter was successfully resolved in 1960, whereupon Rangoon enjoyed improved relations with China until the Cultural Revolution. Then, however, local agitation by Chinese diplomats and the overseas Chinese community prompted anti-Chinese riots that led bilateral ties into decline. Ne Win sought to manage the relationship in part by signalling an improvement in ties with India in the late 1960s, and before too long, by dint of the antagonism in Sino-Soviet relations, found Beijing prepared to develop more positive ties. However, Burma was obliged to accept Beijing's military and political support to the Communist Party of Burma (CPB) that only ended in the 1980s. This demonstrated that external and internal security were indivisible.

After 1962, Burma's commitment to non-alignment and isolation from the outside world until the 1970s also reflected the Ne Win regime's view that the country's formal independence had not led to 'real' independence, understood as involving the resurrection of 'traditional Burma'.[11] In the words of historian Michael Aung-Thwin, '[t]he country needed "time with itself", an uninterrupted period in which some of the traditional values, and the structural and ideological principles that had shaped Burmese society in the pre-colonial past, could be resurrected'.[12] This also necessitated national control of the country's economic assets.

Contestation over the legitimacy of the regime and its policies had sparked a communist insurrection soon after independence. In addition, the country simultaneously faced a series of ethnic insurgencies that developed as the government pursued the objective of building for the first time in Burma's history an integrated polity comprising both the Burman majority and the ethnic nationalities. This was complicated by the fact that the 1947 Constitution established a federal framework that did not address the concerns of the Karen (Kayin), Mon and Arakanese, whereas it offered the Shan State and Kayah State the right to secede from the Union after ten years, upon which aggrieved ethnic nationalists went underground. The state's problems of legitimacy were compounded when the U Nu government failed to act on the vision of the Burmese nationalist leader Aung San, who had promised the minorities an equitable share of the country's wealth. The ethnic nationalities responded angrily to a perceived erosion of their local autonomy by the army's state-building activities. The 1962 military coup was, in turn, justified in part as necessary to prevent the civilian government from allowing the state to disintegrate in response to demands for more substantive federalism.[13] Dealing with the armed, Beijing-supported communist as well as ethnic insurgencies constituted the chief security concern for Ne Win's regime.[14] However, by 1987 not only had the creation of a strong and unified state eluded Ne Win, but the Burmese Way to Socialism had also proved so economically flawed in practice that irrespective of its resource wealth the country found itself reclassified as a least-developed country.[15]

Changing foreign policy context

Myanmar's external environment has changed radically since the end of the 1980s. Then, China's withdrawal of support for the CPB helped remove a major element of external threat. Myanmar's external relations nevertheless remained difficult, particularly given Western states' vilification of the military government and the fact that the brutal nature of the restoration of order in 1988–90 meant that former donor countries were no longer prepared to offer development assistance. Neighbours, particularly Thailand, offered sanctuaries to anti-regime forces and ethnic insurgents. Subsequently, during the 1990s China's good-neighbourly policy, the trend towards peace and reconciliation in Southeast Asia, as well as moves towards regional and sub-regional economic cooperation involving China, ASEAN and India have transformed Myanmar's immediate habitat. Positive developments in its external affairs landscape notwithstanding, Myanmar's overall external foreign-policy environment has remained extremely challenging. Meanwhile, though over time 17 ceasefires have been agreed between the military government and a series of both smaller and more formidable ethnic insurgent armies, armed conflict with several ethnic-minority organisations has continued.[16] The military also continues to face opposition from various anti-regime and pro-democracy forces.

The political-security imperative

Myanmar's military officially pursues the so-called 'Three Main National Causes' (non-disintegration of the Union, non-disintegration of national solidarity, the perpetuation of the country's sovereignty) and 12 'National Objectives' in the political, economic and social spheres.[17] Capturing what may be summed up as the core of the military's domestic political-security imperative, the Three Main National Causes highlight the continued danger of Myanmar breaking up. As the military government itself has over the years claimed to have initiated a successful ceasefire policy and achieved important military victories over ethnic insurgents, it might seem that the regime is exaggerating domestic threats to national unity and stability for its own purposes. While this may be true to a limited extent, given that there is no clear distinction between security for the state, the regime and the military government,[18] there remain significant challenges to state-building. 'Non-ceasefire' groups still pose a military and political challenge and, more importantly perhaps, there are myriad difficulties in moving beyond the ceasefire arrangements in an inclusive manner.[19] Having allowed the ceasefire groups to retain their arms, to police their own territory and to maintain their security forces to protect both legal and illegal business activities, the distinct possibility remains that the military government will fail to persuade all of the often fiercely autonomously minded ethnic nationalities to embrace the idea of a unitary state and to lay down their weapons, as they are expected to do by the time of the signing of a new constitution. The status quo in itself is not necessarily conducive to the project of an integrated state. According to one assessment, for instance, the 'Wa region for most intents and purposes today is an independent state and has much closer links with China than with the rest of Myanmar'.[20]

The military regime sees itself as being the only institution capable of bringing to an end the momentous task of state-building that began with independence. In attempting to do so, the military believes that the centrifugal aspirations of the ethnic minorities do not allow for a return to the spirit of the Panglong Conference at which Aung San's government-in-waiting, in order to win independence from Britain, exchanged with the participating ethnic nationalities guarantees of autonomy in return for the acceptance of a Union of Burma; the 1947 Constitution is not an option for the SPDC. Consequently, the military has consistently cried foul whenever the NLD has seemed intent on reinstating failed forms of federalism. The military believes that for its project of state-building to succeed, it is necessary to set up what is, in essence, a centralised unitary state, even if the constitution still being drawn up by the NC will nevertheless include federal-style provisions.[21]

The SPDC logic in seeking to secure an enduring constitution, later to be ratified by referendum, as a precursor to democratic elections is apparently that it will likely be impossible to achieve this constitution under the norms of democracy. Instead, it is necessary to forge a deal coercively. In other words, the domestic political-security imperative also involves first addressing the question of power sharing with the ethnic groups and denying a transition to democracy that could easily lead to the unravelling of what has thus far been attained. The military is thus planning for a transition to 'national democracy' or 'discipline-flourishing democracy', which to the regime stands for the abandonment of armed struggle and thus is to be distinguished from liberal democracy.[22] Given the perceived uncertainties of party politics, the military's argument is indeed also that, even with a new constitution in place, the military is to continue to play an overt role and the exercise of executive power is to be removed from competitive politics. Assigning the completion of state-building priority over democratisation is politically controversial, especially to those keen on advancing regime change in Myanmar. However, it does reflect the political experience of other states, and there is a strong argument that without agreed power sharing, '[it] would [for example] be virtually impossible for a democratic government [to] ... collect taxes or implement social or economic policy in ... the Kokang region'.[23]

From the regime's perspective, national solidarity is a prerequisite for successful state-building. The SPDC has hence argued consistently that all national races share the common goals of stability, peace and national development within a unified state. In practice, it has supported multi-sectoral development programmes in ethnic-minority areas benefiting from cease-fire agreements. However, development in itself and the growing reach of the military has continued to present challenges including internal displacement. The appeal to national solidarity has thus far not obscured the fact that the limited progress in dealing with the ethnic question is part of the wider malaise of Myanmar's politics that has in part been attributed to 'institutional intolerance for any form of dissent' and involves entrenched suspicion and fear.[24]

The third aspect of the military's political-security imperative – the perpetuation of sovereignty – is best understood against the backdrop of history. At its core is Myanmar's experience of colonial subjugation by the British, who, in the late nineteenth century, deposed Burma's King Thibaw and uprooted a whole social and economic order.[25] The colonial experience accounts for strong and pervasive nationalism and the leadership's collective hypersensitivity to all perceived threats of interference.[26] If there is one clear message that Myanmar's government broadcasts consistently, then this is that the country will resist what it perceives as 'attempts to subjugate Myanmar' or 'neo-colonial politics'. Some suggest that the leadership has a 'siege mentality bordering on paranoia'.[27] Be that as it may, sovereignty is a basic value that the military is keen to defend.

Foreign policy goals

For the *Tatmadaw*, national security policy denotes 'a policy that a nation has laid down in order to avoid, prevent and manipulate the dangers, both from the internal and external threats on its political, military, economical and other affairs'.[28] External and internal national security are inter-related, with operational emphasis on counter-insurgency.[29] In this context, Myanmar's defence policy emphasises 'active defence' against lower-level external military threats.[30] There is a system of total people's defence in which the *Tatmadaw*, with its limited conventional military capability, is the primary line of defence,[31] to be supplemented in the event of likely defeat by auxiliary forces engaging in guerrilla warfare along Maoist lines.[32] The purpose of Myanmar's foreign-policy, meanwhile, is to respond to, manage and influence the country's external environment, and to promote the military's domestic goals. Officials have identified a clear hierarchy of core foreign-policy objectives: first, to enhance the country's security; second, to bolster the nation's economic development and prosperity; and, third, to promote a peaceful and equitable world order.[33]

To serve the domestic political-security imperative, foreign policy has, for instance, focused on persuading neighbours to adopt clearer policies of non-interference in order to reduce the *Tatmadaw's* confrontations with ethnic insurgents along the borders. The SLORC/SPDC has also been much concerned about external actors who seek to interfere in the internal affairs of the state.[34] Indeed, the military regards the slander of the government, the incitement to social unrest and cyber-terrorism as key threats to security, stability and the existing social order.[35] Consequently, foreign policy has attempted to repulse the security challenge inherent in the international support for ASSK.

The foreign policy of the SLORC/SPDC has also served to satisfy Myanmar's development needs as part of the state-building project.[36] Having squandered substantial international development assistance and been disqualified after 1988 from receiving assistance such as soft loans from international financial institutions, the country's foreign policy has served to promote economic cooperation with neighbouring economies to supplement national development.[37] This has involved promoting border trade, offering incentives to tap into private foreign capital and requesting technical and other development assistance, while decrying the impact of economic sanctions. Above all, Myanmar has sought assistance and investment to enhance its infrastructure and to support oil and gas exploration and extraction, from which the government hopes to benefit substantially. Myanmar has also pursued policies of sub-regional economic integration.[38]

The goal of promoting a peaceful and equitable world order has traditionally been pursued within the United Nations and the military believes that it has a particular diplomatic contribution to make on the disarmament front. Myanmar favours both general and nuclear disarmament and it has expended a great deal of energy to keep the issues of disarmament and non-proliferation alive within the multilateral framework of the UN. However, leaders and officials also emphasise that since independence their country has never interfered in the internal affairs of another state, while also standing for peace and non-aggression in line with Buddhist scriptures.

Beyond security, foreign policy can also serve to win international recognition, which in turn is regarded as helping to legitimise the regime at home, even if it can already claim some legitimacy on the basis of cognitive models that permeate social practices, domestic unpopularity notwithstanding.[39] In stark contrast to foreign perspectives, the regime sees itself standing in the line of meritorious rulers who have ultimately succeeded in forging national unity.[40] The search for international recognition has seen Myanmar seek membership of regional institutions and to some extent also probably driven efforts to embrace political change at home,[41] but Myanmar's foreign-policy priority is clear. The basic security imperative has consistently been regarded as more important than the goals of development or improved international standing.

ASSK as a foreign-policy challenge

While to many she represents the face of human rights and democracy in Burma, the regime has regarded ASSK as an annoyance and menace. Some even argue that in line with cultural images of the past she has been regarded by the military as a modern incarnation of a contender to the throne (*minlaung*) and hence as a supreme threat to its hold on power.[42]

ASSK has represented a foreign-policy challenge in that, as an icon of democracy and freedom as well as a Nobel Prize laureate, she has become an important focal point for other countries' foreign policy towards Myanmar. This applies to the United States, the United Kingdom and other European countries, as well as to Japan, to varying degrees. Her trenchant criticisms of the regime have strongly influenced the policy of Western states towards Myanmar, leading them to intensify pressure on the military to step aside. Her opposition to Myanmar receiving comprehensive development aid has for years been a decisive factor in Japan largely limiting its donor activities to humanitarian assistance. When she has been placed under house arrest, foreign governments have applied pressure on Myanmar to release ASSK immediately and unconditionally. These demands, and the refusal to accede to them, have cost Myanmar much of its international reputation. When released from house arrest, ASSK has repeatedly resorted to acts of political provocation to protest both against the nature of political rule and the curtailment of her rights, not least her freedom of movement, in the apparent hope that such actions will galvanise international public opinion and sufficiently embarrass the junta to force political change. For example, she undertook several attempts (one of which coincided with the ASEAN Ministerial Meeting [AMM]) to leave Yangon by car in July and August 1998, which twice left her stranded at Anyarsu in her vehicle for days. She and other NLD leaders also irritated the regime in 1998 by deciding to form the Committee Representing the People's Parliament (elected in 1990), which included seven elected members and three unelected members (including herself), and to declare invalid all legislation passed after 18 September 1988.[43] The SPDC initiated a massive crackdown against the NLD, which in turn produced more international condemnation. Timed to coincide more or less with the UN Millennium Summit, ASSK and NLD Vice-Chairman U Tin Oo, in late August 2000, provoked the regime into again placing ASSK under de facto house arrest, despite the considerable international outcry this was bound to engender.

Following her renewed release in May 2002, the SPDC again found itself confronting international pressure to begin a genuine dialogue with ASSK. This pressure increasingly conflicted with the regime's political-security imperative because, contrary to an apparently tacit understanding reached that year between her and the authorities, over time ASSK used travel opportunities to draw huge crowds in the countryside as if she was already campaigning for office. When her activities eventually proved unbearable to the regime, she was forcefully detained and taken into 'protective custody'. The violence of the Depayin incident of 30 May 2003, where at least four people died, led to a huge international outcry directed at the military regime, followed by even harsher unilateral sanctions imposed by the West. In short, unable to ignore her perceived provocations, the military regime has found that its actions against ASSK have set back its relations with Western countries substantially. Even as Western countries have begun to emphasise the deterioration of human rights in ethnic-minority areas in order to secure UNSC scrutiny of the situation in Myanmar, ASSK's house arrest and the regime's refusal to engage her in a genuine political dialogue remain major obstacles to improved relations with Western countries and Japan.

Location and assets

Faced with Western opprobrium and sanctions, Myanmar has above all relied on its location and resources to attract and sustain the interest of neighbouring countries in developing economic and political ties. The country shares land boundaries with Bangladesh (271km) and India (1338km) to the west, China in the north (2204km), as well as Laos (238km) and Thailand (2107km) in the east and southeast.[44] Myanmar's leaders appreciate that given its location as the bridge between South, Southeast and East Asia, the country has long been deemed strategically important. Britain, as the colonial power, regarded Rakhine as critical to safeguarding eastern India, while the Tanintharyi was key to protecting entry into the Malacca Strait. During the Second World War, Burma became a major theatre of operations as the Allies strove to support the Chinese Nationalist forces in the Anti-Japanese War. During the early Cold War, Myanmar was regarded as a springboard to re-penetrating Communist China.[45] More recently, the authorities in Yunnan Province and China's central government have seen Myanmar as providing both a hinterland for trade and a strategic outlet to the Bay of Bengal. For India, Myanmar holds the key to peace in the northeast and closer physical links with Southeast Asia. Myanmar's geostrategic significance has for years also featured in discussions over Sino-Indian rivalry.[46] For Thailand, Myanmar is the door to South Asia.

The military regime clearly sees the opportunities afforded by its geographical position in the context of efforts to establish a modern and integrated state. It has largely reacted favourably to its neighbours' interest in enhancing the country's infrastructure in the knowledge that this will increase its geoeconomic and geopolitical significance and serve its own interests. The regime can also capitalise on its natural resources (timber, with exports of US$300 million in 2003–04, as well as minerals and fish) to attract its neighbours' interest in economic cooperation. Above all, the Myanmar government hopes to generate substantial income through the export to neighbours of natural gas, with the likely combined 2005 revenue from existing offshore gas fields (Yadana and Yetagun) estimated at more than US$250m set to rise.[47] Substantial gas fields have also been discovered off the Rakhine coast. The government has also benefited from its location in that neighbours have regarded its participation in sub-regional economic cooperation schemes as vital. By 2005, Myanmar was tellingly not only a member of ASEAN, the ASEAN Regional Forum (ARF), ASEAN+3 (consisting of ASEAN and China, Japan and South Korea) and the inter-regional Asia–Europe Meeting (ASEM), but also several sub-regional forums including Bangladesh, India, Myanmar, Sri Lanka and Thailand-Economic Cooperation (BIMST-EC),[48] the Greater Mekong Sub-region (GMS) Development Programme, the Indian-floated Ganga-Mekong Cooperation Programme and the Thai-initiated Ayeyawady-Chao Phraya-Mekong

Economic Cooperation Strategy involving Cambodia, Laos, Myanmar, Thailand and Vietnam. As the former general director of the Ministry of Foreign Affairs's Political Department put it, '[Myanmar] cannot hope to attain its national goals and objectives by staying isolated and not drawing upon the resources and advantages of regional cooperation'.[49]

Conclusion

Myanmar's foreign policy reflects both the country's domestic conditions – its insecurity and weakness and the military's prescription to overcome these – as well as the nature of and change in its external environment. With the country still grappling with ethnic insurgencies, the SPDC is eager to advance a state-building project that goes back to the dawn of independence, while attempting to take advantage of both its geographical location and resources in attracting external assistance and backing. Myanmar's foreign policy stands in continuity with the past in that the SPDC emphasises the importance of an independent and active foreign policy. This implies creating and maintaining as much manoeuvrability in its foreign relations with neighbouring powers as possible, while resisting threats to its sovereignty.

CHAPTER TWO

Myanmar's Foreign Policy towards China and India

Myanmar has benefited substantially from the development of its relations with its two giant neighbours, China and India. While from 1988 the SLORC looked to Beijing to satisfy its immediate need for political support, military assistance and trade, in more recent years the focus has been on diplomatic support and assistance with Myanmar's industrial and infrastructural development. Myanmar's ties with India have improved only more recently, since New Delhi re-evaluated its foreign policy towards Yangon in the mid-1990s. Although since independence there has never been a time when Yangon's relations with both Beijing and New Delhi have been simultaneously as good, Khin Nyunt's political departure in 2004 ignited speculation over whether Myanmar would begin to lean more towards India.

Myanmar–China relations

In 1988, the SLORC looked to China for regime support and economic cooperation in the knowledge that Beijing accorded Myanmar strategic significance in light of Deng Xiaoping's policies of opening up and economic reform, particularly from the perspective of the neighbouring Chinese province of Yunnan. The SLORC's approach to China occurred despite lingering perceptions of threat, not least because China had, until the mid-1980s, provided extensive military and political support to the CPB, allowing the Burmese communists to sustain the most formidable insurgency campaign among all insurrectionist groups. Momentum towards better relations with China gathered pace with the disintegration of the CPB in early 1989 and the Tiananmen incident in June that year, which brought the domestic and international predicaments faced by the SLORC and the Chinese Communist Party into closer alignment.[1]

Yangon's decision to turn to China for assistance delivered almost immediate benefits. First, China deflected Western human-rights criticisms targeting Myanmar. At the United Nations General Assembly (UNGA) in 1990, Beijing prevented the adoption of the first-ever draft resolution on the human-rights situation in Myanmar (but thereafter fell into line, allowing future draft resolutions to be adopted by consensus). Second, an initial border trade agreement reached in 1988 paved the way for substantial economic exchange with China. Following Than Shwe's visit to China in October 1989, Chinese and particularly Yunnanese state companies began to play major parts in the economic reconstruction of northern Myanmar, especially by building power stations, roads, bridges and telecommunication facilities. In return, Myanmar agreed to the exploitation by Chinese companies of natural resources in the ethnic-minority areas along the border. Third, two substantial arms deals with China in 1990 and 1994, worth about US$1.2 billion and US$400m respectively,[2] allowed the *Tatmadaw* to replenish and upgrade its armaments for counter-insurgency operations and conventional war-fighting on land and sea. Weapons supplied included heavy artillery, multiple rocket launchers, patrol boats, guided missile attack craft, fighter aircraft, air-to-air missiles, electronic warfare and signals intelligence (SIGINT) equipment, as well as night vision equipment.[3] When Premier Li Peng visited in 1994, the SLORC referred to China as its 'most trusted friend'. China had undoubtedly contributed greatly to regime survival and growing stability in the early years of the SLORC's rule.

Some external observers took the view that Myanmar was on course to become a 'client state' of China. This assessment was in part based on reports of China delivering and allegedly operating equipment for SIGINT activities on Great Coco Island, Ramree Island off the Rakhine coast, Hainggyi Island at the mouth of the Ayeyarwady Delta, Monkey Point in Yangon and Zadetkyi Kyun off the Kra Peninsula along the Tanintharyi coast, with a view to collecting intelligence on air and naval movements in the eastern parts of the Bay of Bengal and on India's facilities on the Andaman Islands. One further possible objective was to intercept telemetry from Indian ballistic missile test launches.[4] Some analysts argued that China – beyond providing relevant training – had a continuous presence on Great Coco, the main SIGINT collection facility, in effect making it a 'joint listening station'.[5] Less controversial was the claim that improvements to maritime surveillance capabilities had allowed Myanmar's military to obtain by 1994 a relatively comprehensive picture of activity in its waters.[6] Myanmar and China negotiated a military cooperation agreement in 1996 containing provisions for intelligence exchanges.[7]

The view of Myanmar as China's client state was also based on claims of Chinese involvement in massive civil and military development projects, including the upgrading of airstrips and ports, that it was believed could potentially serve as forward operating bases for the People's Liberation Army Navy (PLA[N]) and even support a permanent Chinese military presence in future. Although there is no doubt that Myanmar invested in the development of new and existing military facilities, the extent of China's involvement is unclear. Andrew Selth has suggested that many claims regarding China's role in modernising Myanmar's strategic infrastructure have been incorrect and probably 'planted by self-interested parties'.[8] Certainly, claims that naval facilities might henceforth be used by the PLA(N) to protect sea lanes of communication to the Middle East or to dominate the approach to the Malacca Strait would appear to have been no more than speculation. Chinese officials have routinely denied having bases or permanent deployments in Myanmar, while Myanmar officials have repeatedly indicated that they would not allow foreign bases in line with their independent and active foreign policy. Notably, expressions of concern especially from Indian analysts have become less shrill in recent years.[9] The United States government has equally remained quiet on the issue, indicating perhaps that alarmist interpretations of Myanmar–China defence cooperation lack credibility, although more recent internal reports apparently see Myanmar as playing a part in what has been dubbed China's 'string of pearls' strategy, the purpose of which would be to protect Beijing's energy interests and to promote its wider geopolitical and security interests.[10]

Indeed, evidence abounds that Myanmar was eager to avoid undue military, political or economic dependence on China. The regime quickly diversified its sources of weapons procurement, as illustrated by the purchase from Russia of helicopter gunships in 1995 and 10 second-hand MiG-29s in 2001. Myanmar also developed defence relationships with Israel, Pakistan and Singapore.[11] Myanmar has broadened its arms supply sources to include India, North Korea, Serbia and Ukraine.[12] And while they continue, purchases of Chinese military equipment are no longer on the scale seen in the early 1990s, although observers in

2004 speculated that a further major arms deal was being negotiated.[13] Price has also been an issue. Lacking funds to acquire complete naval vessels to patrol national waters and to protect maritime resources, the SPDC only bought hulls from China, for subsequent fitting out domestically as corvettes.[14]

On the political level, Myanmar's leaders may effectively have recognised China as its 'senior' in their *paukphaw* (cousin, literally 'one womb away') relationship, but they have also continued nevertheless to stress the Five Principles of Peaceful Coexistence, emphasising sovereign equality and non-interference. This suggests that Myanmar's leaders are interested in good working relations with China, but suspicious of its long-term strategic intentions. And to diversify its sources of diplomatic support, the regime has focused on developing bilateral relations with India, Thailand, other ASEAN members, as well as Russia.

Fears about possible future Chinese economic domination also seem to have spurred Yangon to enhance economic ties with ASEAN states.[15] At least during the early to mid-1990s, when Myanmar demonstrated a respectable economic performance and was able to attract foreign direct investment (FDI) from various ASEAN and Western countries, SPDC leaders appear to have been confident that the military would be able to balance or dilute Chinese influence.[16] In the wake of the 1997 Asian financial crisis, however, China's importance as an economic and political-security partner again increased in relative terms. This reflected the deterioration in Myanmar's external environment, which after 1997 was characterised not only by the continued refusal of international financial institutions to provide development assistance, but also by a tighter US sanctions regime, the withdrawal under public and government pressure of FDI by some Western companies and the drop in investment from the ASEAN countries.

The increasing lack of commitment or disregard demonstrated by major powers and to a lesser extent Thailand for the principles of non-interference and non-intervention in the late 1990s also created new uncertainties for the SPDC that reinforced bilateral cooperation with China. For its part, Myanmar observed strict adherence to the One-China principle and offered Beijing moral support in the context of the accidental US attack on China's Belgrade embassy during the Kosovo War in May 1999. However, both sides saw potential for even closer bilateral relations and the Joint Statement on the Framework Document on Future Cooperation, signed by Foreign Ministers U Win Aung and Tang Jiaxuan in June 2000,[17] aimed for closer economic cooperation in the areas of trade, investment, agriculture, fishery, forestry and tourism, as well as agreement to implement accords as soon as possible on border management. Myanmar received a US$120m loan from China in September 2000 to pay for equipment required to generate hydropower. Myanmar increased its cooperation with China on anti-narcotics operations. In 2001 the two sides signed a memorandum of understanding that established a framework for joint operations. Law enforcement cooperation has resulted in numerous renditions of drug traffickers to China. As early as October 2000, Myanmar had signed the ASEAN and China Cooperative Operations in Response to Dangerous Drugs scheme; the following year it started to participate in ministerial-level drug-control talks also involving Laos and Thailand.

Economic and development cooperation
Undertaken as part of a broader Chinese charm offensive towards Southeast Asia,[18] Chinese President Jiang Zemin's 2001 visit to Myanmar breathed new life into bilateral economic relations. By late 2002, Chinese companies had officially contracted more than 800 projects with a total value of US$2.1bn.[19] In January 2003 Than Shwe visited China again, securing a US$200m preferential loan to finance construction of one of Myanmar's largest planned hydropower projects, at Yewya near Mandalay.[20] Days later, China agreed to remit part of Myanmar's overdue debt. In August 2003, Myanmar signed a contract worth US$150m for the Shweli hydroelectric power project in Northern Shan State.[21] In March 2004, Myanmar leaders and visiting Chinese Vice-Premier Madam Wu Yi signed further memorandums of understanding, including agreements on mineral exploration along the Myanmar–China border region and the Lashio–Muse railroad project.[22] Visiting China in July 2004, Khin Nyunt exchanged notes on the construction of an international convention centre, master plans for hydropower projects in Myanmar and the Thanlyin–Kyauktan Industrial Zone. Notably, his Chinese interlocutors impressed upon Khin Nyunt the advantages of moving towards more radical economic reform. Myanma Oil and Gas Enterprise (MOGE) has signed onshore oil production-sharing contracts with China National Petrochemical Corporation and China National Offshore Oil Corporation, which has also acquired a stake in three blocks awarded for exploration (Rakhine Block A-4 and Moattama Blocks M-2 and M-10). It would have gained a 28% stake in the Yadana project had its bid for Unocal succeeded.[23] At the Second ASEAN–China Business Summit in Nanning in October 2005 Soe Win reiterated Myanmar's hope that its oil and gas

sector (in offshore areas) would be one of three (next to hydroelectric power and manufacturing) attracting additional Chinese investments.

As these examples illustrate, China has assisted Myanmar in a plethora of development projects. China's role in Myanmar's quest to become a diversified energy exporter (thus far, Myanmar's gas exports go to Thailand) is particularly significant, however, as successful exploration will ultimately raise ample foreign currency and strengthen further economic interdependence with China. Having access to Myanmar's gas reserves is also in the interests of China's own energy security. There is now renewed Chinese interest in constructing a pipeline and transport corridor through Myanmar to link Yunnan with the Bay of Bengal, involving the building of a deep-water port in Kyaukphyu on Ramree Island and a 1900-km Kunming–Mandalay–Kyaukphyu road link.[24] Myanmar would thus obtain another strategically important transport artery.[25] Despite Myanmar having long enjoyed considerable strategic significance from China's perspective, not least as a trade outlet to the Bay of Bengal and the Indian Ocean,[26] ambitious ideas such as linking China via Bhamo and the Ayeyarwardy with a deep-sea port on the Bay of Bengal have not been easy to implement.[27] In part, this is because the Ayeyarwardy, though navigable south of Bhamo most of the year, can only really support flat-bottom boats. Moreover, Myanmar still does not possess a deep-sea port. While evidently interested in exploring the proposed transport links, it is clearly beyond Yangon to contribute financially to their realisation in any substantial way.

According to official statistics, China–Myanmar bilateral trade, including border trade, has risen steadily since the Asian crisis. Myanmar continues to import consumer goods, but also machinery and electrical equipment, construction materials and medicines. Timber products and precious stones remain the primary exports to China.[28] In 2002, the official trade volume was US$845m, in 2003, it reached US$1.07bn, in 2004 US$1.145bn and in 2005 US$1.209bn. Trade with Yunnan Province, also including border trade, apparently stands at US$630mn.

Political and security cooperation

Particularly since the international fallout from the Depayin incident of May 2003, Myanmar's foreign policy has focused once more on maintaining Chinese political-diplomatic backing. Though Chinese officials and policy-makers seem to have speculated that the UN-facilitated process of reconciliation between the SPDC and ASSK might lead to a political settlement, and reportedly privately encouraged a direct approach by ASSK to Than Shwe in 2004 to reduce political tensions,[29] since her renewed detention and subsequent house arrest Myanmar has found Beijing to be very supportive in public. China bolsters Myanmar's efforts to safeguard national independence and sovereignty, opposes foreign interference in Myanmar's internal affairs, and believes that Myanmar's affairs should be resolved by the government and people. When Myanmar and China assumed the roles of co-chairs of the ARF Intersessional Meeting on Confidence-Building shortly after the Depayin incident in July 2003, Beijing helped Myanmar to confront its critics proactively and toned down criticisms of the regime when preparing the co-chairs' statement. China only agreed to participate in the Thai-sponsored 'Bangkok Process' in December 2003, which brought together supposedly 'like-minded countries' for a briefing on the SPDC's seven-point road map, because Myanmar was happy for the event to proceed. Up until the final session of the UN Commission on Human Rights (UNCHR) in March 2006, China continued to speak up for Myanmar, while criticising the concept of country-specific resolutions. China has called on the international community to offer constructive assistance to Myanmar to resolve its domestic issues independently. As Than Shwe has reiterated, Myanmar has been truly appreciative of consistent Chinese support. That said, China has voiced hopes that Myanmar will be able to 'make efforts in speeding up political settlements of existing disputes and move toward democratic progress so as to enhance stability and peaceful development'.[30] In other words, China too wants the SPDC to make more rapid headway with the process of national reconciliation, as this is the precondition for dealing with transnational crime along the border more successfully, to intensify economic exchanges and perhaps to reduce the West's political interest in Myanmar.

In what seems like a *quid pro quo* for China's support, Myanmar has been happy to improve bilateral cooperation in ensuring peace, stability and the development of the border areas, including further efforts towards eliminating narcotics and encouraging the cultivation of opium-substitute crops. For success in this regard, Yangon has itself depended, *inter alia*, on the cooperation of the United Wa State Army (UWSA), which is deeply involved in the narcotics business. Anti-drug cooperation, Chinese officials indicate, is now considered more successful, although the Chinese side would be happy to see Myanmar receive Western assistance in support of further progress and is keen to sign a further agreement with Myanmar on counter-narcotics control cooperation.[31] Meanwhile, Myanmar's cooperative role in multilateral anti-narcotics initiatives with China, Thailand

and Laos is appreciated. In August 2005, following earlier cooperation on curbing the smuggling of precursor chemicals, the two sides reached an agreement whereby the export of ephedrine from China, which is used to make methamphetamines, will be more tightly controlled.[32] Yangon has felt that it has unjustifiably taken the blame for the manufacture of synthetic drugs though the precursor chemicals are not produced in Myanmar. China is the world's largest producer of ephedrine.[33]

Myanmar and China after the fall of Khin Nyunt

The removal of Khin Nyunt in October 2004 did not alter Myanmar's foreign policy towards China significantly. The fact that Than Shwe travelled to India so shortly afterwards initially raised the possibility that Myanmar might in future wish to privilege relations with New Delhi over those with Beijing. There is no evidence for this, however. Ties with China remain crucial to the support of the SPDC's core foreign-policy goals. Military diplomacy and security cooperation have continued.[34] Since his appointment in October 2004 Soe Win has twice attended the ASEAN–China Business Summit, has represented Myanmar at the Second GMS Summit,[35] and has also promoted bilateral relations with China by making an extended visit in February 2006 that served to strengthen economic and political cooperation, as illustrated by plans to establish new Special Economic Zones in Myanmar and to step up cooperation in energy and resource extraction. China's staunch support for Myanmar has also not changed.

Beijing favoured Myanmar taking on the 2006–07 ASEAN chairmanship and in 2005 began helping Yangon to prepare the necessary infrastructure (especially the extension of the airport and the construction of a new convention centre) to support the summit proceedings. China believed that staying firm on the chairmanship was a necessary demonstration of Myanmar's sovereignty and its ability to resist pressure, while the organisation of the summit would enhance its international image. This suggestion built very much on China's own experience of rebuilding its post-Tiananmen reputation. In the event, though, the SPDC leaders felt obliged to dismiss Beijing's advice on this matter. In June 2005, China voiced its objection to the US attempt to place Myanmar on the UNSC agenda. In what was described as a 'gesture of camaraderie',[36] Chinese Foreign Minister Li Zhaoxing even missed the 12th ARF in Vientiane in favour of a short visit to Yangon, where he met separately with Than Shwe and Soe Win in what was the first visit by a Chinese foreign minister as head of delegation for 13 years.

Though perhaps in part focused on reassuring Myanmar, the visit was also about seeking reassurances from Yangon. In particular, China was keen to hear that Yangon was not endorsing the G-4 proposal intended to help Japan, India, Germany and Brazil to win permanent seats on the UNSC. Beijing had, in particular, been opposed to Tokyo's UNSC membership, on the grounds that it has yet to adopt the correct attitude towards historical issues. As part of Myanmar's drive towards closer relations with India, Than Shwe had endorsed India's bid for UNSC membership the previous October, but since then no official word had passed on Myanmar's stance on UN reform. As the Chinese found, Myanmar's decision-makers would not support the G-4. This was in conformity with China's own position, but the incident was significant in that it indicated that Myanmar remains keen to pursue an independent foreign policy. In what would be a significant diplomatic commitment, Soe Win's visit to China in February 2006 apparently yielded an assurance by Beijing that it would in principle oppose moves to discuss Myanmar at the UNSC. The regime reportedly also asked Beijing for its help in obtaining a similar assurance from Russia.[37]

Myanmar's foreign policy towards China has been extremely effective overall. China's support has helped the SPDC to strengthen its hold on power significantly, while its substantial development assistance has allowed Myanmar to circumvent Western and Japanese sanctions. Myanmar has so far sought to construct mutually beneficial ties with China, while preserving its sovereignty and freedom of action. This is to be achieved by also enhancing economic and political-military relations with India and Russia. Though some impatience with SPDC reforms and concern over the significant transnational challenges originating from Myanmar is palpable in Beijing, particularly where narcotics are concerned, there would appear to be few scenarios in which China would stop offering solid diplomatic support to the regime. Still, Myanmar's decision-makers probably appreciate that with China being asked by the United States to act responsibly as a 'stakeholder' in international society,[38] continued full Chinese support at the UNSC cannot be taken for granted and may come at a price.

Foreign policy towards India

When the SLORC assumed power in 1988, relations with India were essentially cool and disinterested. In line with Burma's policy of non-alignment, Ne Win had rejected once more the idea of Burma joining the South Asian Association for Regional Cooperation, which Indian Prime Minister Rajiv

Gandhi discussed when visiting Rangoon in 1987. That visit in itself had brought little warmth to a relationship that had been frosty since the 1962 military takeover. Indeed, the nationalisation of ethnic Indian commercial interests under the policies of the Burmese Way to Socialism (in 1963) had considerably burdened bilateral ties.[39] The events of 1988 led India to strongly criticise Burma's new military rulers. New Delhi offered refuge to anti-SLORC dissidents and openly sided with democracy activists. Indian support for ASSK built on the fact that she had attended high school in India in the 1960s when her mother was ambassador in New Delhi and made many friends in the Indian political elite. To Myanmar's dismay, in 1991 India released Soe Myint, who was one of two Burmese nationals implicated in the hijacking of a Thai jet on its way to Kolkata in November 1990.[40] The Indian government also permitted the opposition National Coalition Government of the Union of Burma (NCGUB) to open an office in New Delhi in July 1992. Yangon saw these steps as blatant interference in Myanmar's internal affairs. However, the military government lacked obvious trump cards to oblige New Delhi to reconsider its stance, which was part of a moralistic policy of Gandhian and Nehruvian provenance.

By 1993, however, India had itself begun to reassess its policy towards Yangon. Several factors accounted for this change. First, India had apprehensions about a possible encirclement by China and pro-Chinese regimes in Pakistan and Bangladesh, as well as Myanmar. It also fretted about the possibility of China establishing a presence in the Bay of Bengal and Andaman Sea. Second, economic and strategic interests coalesced in New Delhi's 'Look East Policy' under incoming Prime Minister P.V. Narasimha Rao. Third, India sought urgently to address its security problems in the northeast.[41] As a result, India decided to place security and economic objectives ahead of political and human-rights considerations when dealing with Yangon. Following a groundbreaking visit by Foreign Secretary J.N. Dixit to Yangon in 1993, a military dialogue was agreed, as were various institutional links to address transnational challenges including anti-drug and anti-insurgency cooperation. There were some temporary setbacks. In 1995, for instance, the SLORC punished India's decision to honour ASSK with the prestigious Jawaharlal Nehru Award for International Understanding by suspending counter-insurgency cooperation.[42] Myanmar's reaction had the desired effect, however, for within a year India's Foreign Affairs Minister Pranab Mukherjee explicitly designated Myanmar's movement for democracy an 'internal matter'.

Since the second half of the 1990s, Myanmar has actively sought political and military exchanges and economic cooperation with India. Within

Myanmar, Maung Aye has played a crucial role in working towards improved ties with New Delhi. At his invitation, Indian Vice-President Shri Bhairon Singh Shekhawat visited Myanmar in early November 2003 (he was then the highest-ranking Indian leader to visit Myanmar since Rajiv Gandhi in 1987). In October 2004, Than Shwe visited India as Myanmar's head of state, the first high-level visit since that of U Ne Win in 1984.[43] President A.P.J. Abdul Kalam reciprocated by embarking on a state visit in March 2006, the first ever to Myanmar by an Indian head of state. These visits have been supplemented by high-ranking reciprocal exchanges between ministers and military leaders.[44]

Benefiting from relations with India

Myanmar has pursued several inter-related foreign policy interests in its developing relationship with India. These can be summarised as seeking an Indian contribution to economic development, security and political support and even the country's international standing. Positive developments have occurred in all areas since the mid-1990s and especially under the two coalition governments led by the Bharatiya Janata Party of Atal Bihari Vajpayee (1998–2004). Since border trade was legalised, bilateral trade has grown strongly although the volume of formal trade remains less than half of that with China. Official trade, which rose substantially after 2000, stood at US\$486.59m in 2004.[45] From Yangon's perspective, trade with India is particularly important because it is one of the few countries with which Myanmar has a considerable surplus. India is already Myanmar's fifth-largest trading partner after Thailand, China, Singapore and the EU, as well as its third largest export market after Thailand. The main exports from Myanmar are beans, pulses and hardwood, with imports dominated by iron, steel and pharmaceuticals. A second border checkpoint that opened in January 2004 is expected to boost trade further, with the two sides targeting total trade worth US\$1bn in 2006. Notably, Myanmar has also been able to join Indian initiatives for sub-regional economic and tourism integration: Bangladesh, India, Sri Lanka, Thailand-Economic Cooperation, which upon Yangon's accession in December 1997 renamed itself BIMST-EC; and Mekong-Ganga Cooperation, announced in July 2000.[46]

Myanmar has, moreover, succeeded in winning India as a limited source of credit and capital in its quest to build an integrated, stronger and more secure state. After providing minor lines of credit from 1998, in 2003 India provided a US\$56.35m soft loan for the upgrading of the Yangon–Mandalay rail link. Ultimately, the idea is to establish a connecting rail link to Guwahati in India. In 2001 Indian Foreign Minister Jaswant Singh inaugurated the Indian-built 160km Tamu–Kalewa–Kalemyo highway as part of a project intended to link Moreh in Manipur with Mandalay and the Thai border at Mae Sot. India also plans to assist with the upgrading of cross-border roads Rhi-Tidim and Rhi-Falam. Other important infrastructure projects on the table include the Tamanthi Hydroelectric Project on the Chindwin River and the Kaladan Multimodal Transport Project, intended to connect the Indian state of Mizoram with the Bay of Bengal and involving the construction of a highway and use of an inland waterway to Sittwe, which has been developed as a major seaport. There is apparently also interest in constructing a deep-sea port at Dawei in the Tanintharyi Division,[47] which might further facilitate Indian trade with Thailand and Southeast Asia.

India has also registered increasingly serious interest in exploiting Myanmar's hydrocarbon resources. In January 2003, state and private Indian companies acquired shares and exploration rights in offshore and onshore blocks respectively.[48] Myanmar, which has requested Indian participation in developing its energy sector, agreed in principle to export natural gas by pipeline running from the Shwe gas field off the Rakhine coast to Kolkata via Bangladesh. An initial trilateral political agreement reached in January 2005 became hostage to India meeting bilateral demands from Dhaka. In December 2005 Myanmar signed a memorandum of understanding with state-owned PetroChina for the sale of 6.5 trillion cubic feet of gas for 30 years from the gas field in question (A-1 Block), leaving the trinational pipeline project's future in doubt.[49] This development has prompted India to focus its attention on a possible alternative pipeline through Mizoram, thus bypassing Bangladesh.

Limited defence cooperation with New Delhi has also yielded some advantages for Myanmar, including officer training places at India's defence academy and, after a long hiatus, the renewed sale of military equipment.Closer military relations are underscored by now regular visits to Myanmar by Indian ships. Myanmar participated in MILAN 2003, a multilateral meeting organised by the Indian Navy to foster confidence-building among Indian Ocean navies. In MILAN 2006, the home-built Myanmar Navy corvette *UMA Anawratha* docked at India's Port Blair in the Andaman Islands. The SPDC is reportedly interested in purchasing from India naval aircraft and anti-aircraft guns.[50] Myanmar has reportedly also proposed that the Indian Navy train its sailors and officers in weapons and sensors, engineering and offshore operations.[51] Meanwhile, after Myanmar's 2001 purchase of a squadron of MiG-29s from Russia, India reportedly agreed to share its expertise in operating Russian equipment.[52]

Improvements in relations with India have boosted Myanmar's international image and legitimacy. India has sustained its pragmatic policy towards Yangon under different governments in New Delhi, including the current Congress-led administration. New Delhi did not issue any statement of concern after the Depayin incident of May 2003. Instead it responded positively when then-foreign minister U Win Aung travelled to India as special envoy of Than Shwe in July 2003 in an apparent bid to explain Myanmar's domestic conditions. India also defended Myanmar at the United Nations Commission on Human Rights. Myanmar has repaid India's political investment in two main ways: first, by conveying full support for India's quest for permanent membership of the UNSC; second, by reiterating and acting on the assurance given by former foreign minister U Win Aung in January 2003 that anti-Indian groups would not be allowed to stage insurgencies from Myanmar's territory. On the occasion of his October 2004 state visit to India, shortly after the forced political departure of Khin Nyunt, Than Shwe again committed Myanmar not only to overcome insurgent activities, but also reaffirmed the regime's willingness to cooperate with India to prevent cross-border crime, including drug-trafficking and arms-smuggling.[53] From late 2004, Myanmar's forces repeatedly engaged in a concerted military campaign against the S.S. Khaplang faction of the National Socialist Council of Nagaland (NSCN).[54] Myanmar's commitment may count for even more if the ceasefire between the Indian government and the NSCN should break down.[55] The SPDC's stance towards Manipuri or Assamese insurgents is, however, considered more ambiguous, as illustrated by the release of Manipuri rebels whose bases were captured in 2001.

In part to assuage the US, which has been critical of New Delhi's position on Myanmar, India has offered Myanmar assistance in building constitutional structures and a democratic polity. This offer was reiterated during Kalam's visit to Myanmar in March 2006.[56] However, even given added expressions of concern for the well-being of ASSK, this offer is very different from New Delhi's outright support for ASSK in the early 1990s. During his visit in March 2005 India's Minister of External Affairs Shri K. Natwar Singh, emphasised that New Delhi attached a 'very high priority to its relations with Myanmar as a valuable neighbour and strategic partner'.[57] In light of predominant Indian interests towards Myanmar, it is issues of security, drug-trafficking, border trade and management, cross-border infrastructure, and energy cooperation that remain at the centre of

New Delhi's dialogue with Naypyidaw. For Myanmar, close relations with India help to offset its reliance on China for political support, economic development and defence assistance. Nonetheless, China's economic presence in Myanmar by far exceeds that of India.

Whither Myanmar–China–India relations?

Myanmar has used its foreign policy towards China and India to enhance its security and development prospects significantly, allowing the SLORC/SPDC to evade the full impact of Western sanctions. Yangon's close relations with China and India have resulted as much from changes in Myanmar's external environment as from an effective foreign policy. Both Beijing and New Delhi recognise Myanmar's strategic significance, neither can do without the active cooperation of the military regime to deal with a host of transnational challenges, and both increasingly regard Myanmar as an asset in their global competition for energy resources. With these stakes in Myanmar, it looks quite unlikely that either China or India can be easily weaned off their policy of full engagement with their military-run neighbour.

Conclusion

Naypyidaw will be eager to continue to develop and deepen the relationship with both China and India. It is likely to continue to benefit further from relations with each power, particularly as both Beijing and New Delhi seem willing to cooperate with one another on many issues, despite the element of strategic competition between them, as illustrated by their agreement on a 'strategic partnership for peace and prosperity' in April 2005 and New Delhi's recent decision to establish its Far Eastern Naval Command at Port Blair in the Andaman Sea.[58] Both China and India see close economic relations with Myanmar as positive for stability and their efforts to improve Myanmar's infrastructure are complementary. A key question is whether Myanmar will want to deepen its relationship with China. Interesting in this regard is the military's resolution in December 2005 to consider supplying China with enormous gas reserves from Block A-1 off the Rakhine coast. The fact that it made this decision just days before a UNSC briefing on Myanmar might indicate that the SPDC believes it disposes of and may need to rely on potentially fungible economic assets to secure China's full diplomatic support in future. As yet, China has been very clear that Myanmar does not pose a threat to international peace and security. While Beijing, not New Delhi, can continue to provide Yangon with protective cover at the

UN, the military evidently believes it is also prudent to signal to Chinese leaders that its relationship with India is strong and getting still stronger, not least to maintain China's incentive for constructive and supportive relations with Myanmar. At the same time, apart from its commercial function, Myanmar's declared willingness to sell gas from Block A-1 to China amounted to a signal that India only has opportunities to miss. In short, Myanmar's foreign policy towards China and India has helped the military to gain a better hand in dealing with each power respectively and with external pressure more broadly. To maintain as much latitude in its foreign policy as possible, the SPDC should, moreover, be expected to deepen its economic and military relationship with Moscow.

CHAPTER THREE

Myanmar and ASEAN

A prominent feature of SLORC/SPDC foreign policy has been the drive to become embedded in Southeast Asia's regional society. Myanmar has benefited from developing relations with the ASEAN countries, not least because these ties have effectively relieved international pressure on the regime and helped to avoid the need to compromise its independent foreign policy. Myanmar has also found, however, that following its admission to the grouping in 1997, relations with ASEAN have yielded fewer economic advantages than expected and, politically, have tended overall to become more rather than less challenging. Deteriorating relations with Thailand overshadowed other aspects of Yangon's cooperation with ASEAN, particularly between early 2001 and mid-2002 before bilateral ties improved again. Following the Depayin incident, both the status of ASSK and the pace of democratisation in Myanmar have moved to centre-stage from ASEAN's perspective, much to the dismay of the SPDC and those governments that, like Singapore or Indonesia, would like to see ASEAN focus elsewhere but find themselves subjected to increasing external political pressure. Dealing with a pricklier ASEAN has meant that Yangon has faced unexpected foreign-policy challenges. The key question emerging in late 2005 and early 2006 was whether Myanmar would succeed in retaining ASEAN's diplomatic support.

Myanmar's road to ASEAN membership

U Ne Win's Burma declined to join ASEAN on its establishment in 1967. That decision was informed by the perception that the association did not qualify as non-aligned because Thailand and the Philippines both allowed US forces to prosecute the Second Indochina War from their military bases. Reflecting greater pragmatism in foreign policy than its predecessor regime, the SLORC first articulated its interest in joining ASEAN in the early 1990s, even though US bases in the Philippines still existed. Myanmar did eventually join ASEAN in 1997, but this was not a foregone conclusion. In the early 1990s, Malaysia was strongly critical of Yangon in view of the crossborder refugee flow into Bangladesh of Muslims from Rakhine State, which the SLORC ostensibly engineered to weed out illegal immigrants. Malaysia consequently also opposed the 1992 Philippine proposal to offer Myanmar ASEAN observer status and a Thai pitch for an invitation to Yangon to attend the 1993 AMM. However, when Bangkok hosted the AMM in 1994, Myanmar was invited as a 'guest', not least because the idea had found political backing from Jakarta, which was worried about increasing Chinese influence in Myanmar.[1]

From the perspective of Myanmar's SLORC, closer association with ASEAN offered important gains in terms of legitimacy. These came on top of benefits derived from ASEAN's informal adoption of a policy of 'constructive engagement' towards Yangon.[2] This approach had its origins in a change in Thai foreign policy under Prime Minister Chatichai Choonhavan in the late 1980s and was subsequently also pursued by Prime Minister Anand Panyarachun and the first government of Chuan Leekpai.[3] From the perspective of Myanmar's leadership, 'constructive engagement' offered three immediate advantages: first, it effectively reinforced the SLORC's normative shield against external criticisms. Espousing an unshakeable belief in the validity of non-interference, the association rejected censure of the regime from its key dialogue partners.[4] Second, 'constructive engagement' denoted a mix of quiet diplomacy and greater economic interaction from which Myanmar stood to benefit economically. Singapore, Malaysia, Thailand and Indonesia invested in a number of economic sectors in the early 1990s. Thailand was particularly interested in restarting and expanding border trade, which had suffered as a consequence of the SLORC's counter-insurgency campaigns.[5] Third, in the context of Western sanctions, closer relations with ASEAN had the potential to reduce Myanmar's growing economic dependence on China.

Myanmar's admission to ASEAN was achieved in the face of significant American and European opposition, which produced a significant regional solidarity effect.[6] In welcoming Myanmar, the other ASEAN governments also ignored letters from ASSK advising members against its admission. Myanmar could fulfil the economic and technical requirements for joining ASEAN. But without the political support given to Myanmar in key Southeast Asian capitals, Yangon would have found its accession to ASEAN more difficult to master. In the event, Kuala Lumpur, as ASEAN chair, was also keen to ensure the emergence of 'One Southeast Asia' in 1997.[7] As such, Myanmar's membership in ASEAN came about because the majority of Southeast Asian states wanted it to happen. For his part, Foreign Minister U Ohn Gyaw indicated Myanmar's willingness to meet the implicit expectations of other ASEAN members regarding both stability within the country and its contribution to regional security when upon joining the association he said that 'Myanmar will strive her best to maintain the harmony of development at both the national and regional levels'.[8]

Myanmar in ASEAN

Although membership represents an important facet of Myanmar's foreign policy, the regime has played a somewhat taciturn role in ASEAN, initially reflecting no doubt a need to learn about and adapt to the workings of Southeast Asia's premier multilateral diplomatic vehicle. This process has been all the more challenging for Yangon because since 1998 ASEAN has sought to enhance intramural economic cooperation and to deepen regional integration. In 2003, this resulted in an agreement to establish an ASEAN community comprising three pillars: the ASEAN Economic Community; the ASEAN Security Community (ASC); and the ASEAN Social and Cultural Community.[9]

Myanmar has backed a vast number of proposals designed to enhance ASEAN cooperation. For instance, it supported the acceleration of the ASEAN Free Trade Area (AFTA) in the wake of the Asian financial crisis. Not surprisingly, the government has particularly welcomed initiatives to overcome the conspicuous socioeconomic divide between the association's original and new members. Myanmar has also hailed the creation and development of ASEAN+3 and expressed enthusiasm for the China–ASEAN FTA. In contrast, since 1998 Yangon has been wary of changes to the normative framework guiding the association's intramural relations. Yet given the continued general consensus within ASEAN until 2005 in favour of non-interference (and consensual decision-making), Myanmar's military regime has also endorsed members' limited efforts to adapt ASEAN's norms and institutions. While not itself contributing to the development of ideas for the ASC, Myanmar did not stand in its way. It accepted without controversy the inclusion of the word 'democratic' in the text of the 2003 Declaration of Bali Concord II.[10] This was notable because the Bali Concord II was the first major ASEAN document to highlight democracy as a goal for the future of Southeast Asia. Yangon has largely left it to other members to repudiate ideas perceived as premature or inappropriate in the context of ASEAN security cooperation (such as an ASEAN peacekeeping force). Myanmar has, moreover, demonstrated good regional citizenship by regularly attending and organising ASEAN meetings. Beyond those pertaining to functional cooperation, Yangon organised the Second AMM on Transnational Crime in June 1999 and the ASEAN+3 Economic Ministers' Meeting of May 2000. In April 2001, Yangon hosted the first informal foreign ministers' retreat in addition to those connected with the annual ministerial meeting. Myanmar joined China in co-chairing two meetings of the ARF Intersessional Support Group on Confidence-Building Measures in November 2003 and April 2004. It has also represented ASEAN at Geneva in arms control and disarmament talks. To participate in Track II meetings, the government established the Myanmar Institute of Strategic and International Studies (ISIS).[11]

Not all expectations met

While Yangon remains committed to the association, its membership and associated economic benefits have to date proved less unambiguously rewarding than initially anticipated. Myanmar's hopes upon joining the association included assistance from the more developed ASEAN members in capacity-building as well as better access for its agricultural products to regional markets, greater FDI from ASEAN member states, more opportunities for developing entrepreneurial expertise and better overall development prospects.[12] However, while FDI from Singapore, Thailand, Malaysia and Indonesia amounted to 50% of the country's total in 1997, the amount decreased significantly because of the Asian economic crisis. FDI inflows failed to pick up even after Southeast Asia had recovered from the crisis, though the reasons for this low level of investment were complex and, arguably, have more to do with the situation in Myanmar.[13] Recent investments in the crucial oil and gas exploration sector have been more associated with Korean, Chinese and Indian companies, although the state-owned Petroleum Authority of Thailand remains a major investor.[14] The Myanmar–ASEAN trade balance also deteriorated in relative terms before improving once again. While the ASEAN states became the largest source of imports, the share of Myanmar's exports to ASEAN as a percentage of total exports dropped from 46.2% to 25.2% between 1991–92 and 2000–01.[15] By 2004, this figure had risen again to 45.8%, with the official trade volume with ASEAN amounting to 47.2% of total trade.[16]

Yangon has found ASEAN able to provide only limited, albeit welcome, assistance not least because the association has historically not provided development funding, in contrast to the EU. However, the regime has profited from the decision by the original members to grant Myanmar (and other new members) preferential tariffs on a range of products on a voluntary and bilateral basis from January 2002. Myanmar has to some extent also benefited from the Initiative for ASEAN Integration (IAI), launched in Singapore in November 2000.[17] It has received assistance in the area of human-resources training and capacity-building from Singapore and Malaysia (and, for a while, also from the Philippines), but arguably not enough given its dire need.[18] At the same time, whether Myanmar has benefited from the ASEAN–Mekong Basin Development Cooperation scheme is unclear. How Myanmar might benefit from the ASEAN Development Fund, established in July 2005, also remains to be seen.[19]

If the economic benefits accruing from membership have proved to be limited, the political dividends have been more evident. ASEAN has, for instance, demonstrated solidarity with Myanmar in regional relations with Europe, arguing for years that progress in inter-regional relations depended on an end to Europe's deliberate exclusion of Myanmar from the frameworks of ASEAN–EU cooperation and the ASEM. More recently, ASEAN stood its ground in supporting a Vietnamese proposal that led to Myanmar finally joining ASEM in October 2004. Support for Myanmar by ASEAN countries has also been forthcoming in the International Labour Organisation (ILO) – where association members have not supported resolutions passed against Myanmar condemning the country's record on forced labour – and the UN General Assembly. ASEAN countries have, however, left Myanmar to defend itself in the ARF, partly for pragmatic reasons, but partly also because ASEAN states too have been concerned about developments in the country. Notably, ASEAN has always remained in control of wording the ARF chairman's statement. ASEAN's solidarity and support have been appreciated by the government.[20]

The SPDC has also appreciated ASEAN governments' broad support for the principle of non-interference despite an emerging understanding that members should introduce greater flexibility into its practice.[21] Myanmar has itself strictly defended non-interference and non-intervention. Deploring the action of NATO against Serbia, U Win Aung told his ASEAN colleagues in 1999: 'A country's affairs should be handled by its own people and international issues should be solved through negotiations and not through military means.'[22] The military leadership was consequently aghast at the UNSC-sanctioned international intervention in East Timor starting in September 1999, which also included individual ASEAN members. When the ASEAN 'Troika', a mechanism designed to deal with situations of common concern likely to disturb regional peace and harmony, was formally agreed in 2000, Yangon only consented because the safeguards put in place – non-interference and consensus – were deemed sufficient to avoid it ever being invoked. Myanmar has nevertheless had little choice but to tolerate thereafter the practice of 'enhanced interaction' whereby ASEAN does not seek to become involved in the domestic politics of members, although their policies or practices with transborder effects may come under scrutiny. In practice, Myanmar's leaders have repeatedly responded positively to expectations that they brief their fellow members in relation to domestic developments.

Myanmar's problems with Thailand

If, by 2002, Myanmar considered its membership in ASEAN to be a relative success, its bilateral ties with Thailand in particular had experienced a serious border crisis. During Chuan Leekpai's second government (1997–2001) Yangon's ties with Bangkok deteriorated against the backdrop of the Asian crisis, as the transboundary effects of Myanmar's domestic problems such as refugees, illegal immigrants and an increasing influx of synthetic drugs became increasing concerns for Thailand. Indeed, in 1998 the Thai government declared the inflow of narcotic drugs to be the principal security threat to the country. The SPDC was annoyed that the Thai government still failed to observe the norm of non-interference, particularly by continuing to allow for a 'buffer-zone' along the border that allowed permitted insurgents to seek sanctuary in Thailand. Yangon reacted with outrage to the way the Thai authorities resolved the 1999 hostage drama at Myanmar's embassy in Bangkok. This saw Thai Deputy Foreign Minister M.R. Sukhumbhand Paribatra escort 'insurgents-cum-terrorists' to the Myanmar–Thai border for release. Considerable further offence was taken when Bangkok's interior minister referred to hostage takers as 'student activists fighting for democracy'.[23] In response, Yangon closed border checkpoints at considerable cost to Thai traders and also revoked fishing licences. The message was apparently effective. When the next hostage drama involving Myanmar insurgents occurred at Ratchaburi hospital in January 2000, Thai commandoes swiftly and resolutely resolved the situation. Bilateral relations remained tense, however, as Chief of the Royal Thai Army (RTA) General Surayud Chulanont started to accuse the SPDC of having imposed insufficient measures to stem a growing flood of methamphetamines into Thailand. Although Myanmar's leaders had been able to benefit from positive relations with previous army chiefs, their difficulties in developing a positive relationship with Surayud, who was much more interested in increasing the professionalism and reputation of the RTA than in continuing its political role and pursuing its economic ventures, not least in Myanmar, exacerbated the bilateral conflict.

Bilateral tensions reached their peak at the very end of the Chuan Leekpai era in early February 2001, when the two sides engaged in a serious armed border confrontation. This followed initial fighting between the *Tatmadaw* and Shan insurgents under the leadership of Colonel Ywet Sit (Yawd Serk) near Ban Pang Noon, which spilled over into Thai territory. Yawd Serk had reconstituted the Shan United Revolutionary Army (SURA) from Khun Sa's Mong Tai Army (MTA) troops who disagreed with the terms of the MTA's unconditional 1996 surrender to the military government (and renamed itself the Shan State Army [SSA]-South).[24] According to Thai accounts, the 2001 border clash was provoked when *Tatmadaw* troops captured a RTA ranger base at Ban Pang Noon. In retaliation, Thailand's Third Army launched a fierce artillery bombardment in which, as some reports indicate, up to 100 Myanmar troops may have died.[25] *Tatmadaw* shells subsequently landed in Sae Mai, Thailand, forcing the evacuation of the town. According to Myanmar accounts, however, *Tatmadaw* troops deployed on E-7 hillock in the Loi Lan area near Tachilek to guard the border town had the previous month refused a Thai demand to abandon their position. After its subsequent capture by SSA-South, the *Tatmadaw* attempted to retake the hillock. While admitting the shelling of SSA-South positions near Mae Sai, Myanmar media denied shelling the town and instead emphasised how a military exchange with the RTA, in support of the Shan insurgents, led to the shelling of nearby Tachilek, resulting in several civilian casualties and fatalities.[26] With troops massing on both sides, the border was closed in mid-February. The 2001 incident was the most serious military confrontation involving the armies of Myanmar and Thailand after Yangon joined ASEAN in 1997.

To the SPDC, these events demonstrated that Thailand had still not abandoned its buffer-zone policy.[27] In its view, the Thai Third Army had provided supporting fire for insurgents and offered the effective use of Thai territory as a staging ground and sanctuary. There was also speculation that the outgoing Chuan Leekpai had given Third Army Commander Lieutenant General Wattanachai Chaimuenwong free rein against Myanmar's troops.[28] The regional army commander had previously favoured a strong stand in favour of defending Thai sovereignty and also taking decisive action against the drug production and trafficking activities of the UWSA, which he saw as waging a proxy war against Thailand, with some *Tatmadaw* officers receiving kickbacks from Wa drug traffickers. It has been suggested that some

Thai generals even considered targeting the UWSA base at Mong Yawn with air strikes, which was becoming the Wa's main production centre of meth-amphetamines and the hub of the crossborder smuggling network.[29]

In incoming Thai Prime Minister Thaksin Shinawatra, however, the SPDC found a partner who, unlike his predecessors, would pursue economic and security interests *vis-à-vis* Myanmar by demonstrating a greater commitment to addressing Yangon's main bilateral grievances. Having committed Thailand to non-interference shortly after his election victory, from February 2001 Thaksin's administration emphasised a policy of 'forward engagement', implying a concentration on boosting Thailand's economic relations with neighbouring countries. But three days into the new tenure, SSA-South troops attacked a Myanmar military post at Palang Luang, live on Thai and international TV. From Yangon's perspective, this represented an attempt to disrupt possible Myanmar–Thai border détente. In the event, crossborder incursions and shelling by insurgent armies and their state backers continued for several months.[30] Bilateral relations suffered further damage in May when two Thai Air Force F-16 fighter aircraft allegedly strayed across the border and one reportedly fired a rocket into the Myanmar border town of Mong Yun.[31] From February to May, Myanmar's state media and government officials vehemently denounced and provoked Thailand, seemingly to convince Thaksin that if Bangkok was hoping for smooth relations with Yangon, it would finally have to fulfil long-standing commitments and be a good neighbour. The tactic worked: from June 2001 normal bilateral relations were slowly restored with Thaksin's decision to visit Yangon.

Appreciating Thaksin's challenge in reversing Bangkok's Myanmar policy and the political constraints under which he was operating, the SPDC leadership emphasised its interest in friendly relations with Thailand. The two sides signed a joint statement in which they reaffirmed respect for the principle of sovereignty and the peaceful settlement of conflicts. Having previously allowed the Myanmar media to belittle the Thai monarchy, Than Shwe offered an important gesture to Than Shwe by highlighting the central role of the monarchy in Thai politics.[32] A memorandum of understanding to cooperate against drugs was also signed, leading to the establishment of three joint 'narcotics suppression coordination states' at major crossing points on the border. The SPDC, however, rejected the Thai idea of joint military patrols along the border. Thai aerial reconnaissance of drug laboratories was made available, but by then, the UWSA had already dispersed its drug production facilities. Meanwhile, Thailand relied on the US Pacific Command for counter-narcotics equipment training, also involving cooperation in counter-narcotics operations between US Special Forces and a new Thai unit created for this purpose, Task Force 399.[33]

Momentum in bilateral ties developed with Khin Nyunt's visit to Bangkok in early September 2001 which produced agreements to lift restrictions on trade and to cooperate on fishing and illegal labour. There was agreement in principle on repatriating refugees back across the border from Thailand on the grounds that Myanmar's civil war had effectively ended.[34] As a testament of much-improved bilateral relations, Khin Nyunt had an audience with King Bhumibol Adulyadej. The same honour was bestowed on Maung Aye when he visited Thailand in April 2002.

The volatility of bilateral relations was highlighted once again, however, when SSA-South succeeded in taking over *Tatmadaw* positions in May 2002, with the RTA apparently providing supporting fire. Significantly, the Thai press reported on the day of the border conflict that Maung Aye had sanctioned a RTA plan to attack Wa drug production sites inside Myanmar, a claim that was vehemently denied by Yangon. This incident and the ensuing war of words induced the outraged SPDC to close border crossings once more, from May until mid-October 2002, seriously disrupting border trade. It was also followed by a major *Tatmadaw* offensive to retake lost positions. Thaksin surprised the Thai public by declaring in late May 2002 that Thailand would henceforth abandon its buffer-zone policy, a step, after all, that Bangkok previously declared to have long taken. Thaksin repeatedly stressed non-interference as part of Thailand's foreign and security policy and insisted that his country must no longer be used for attacks on neighbours. Foreign Minister Surakiart Sathirathai made a fence-mending trip to Yangon in August 2002. Meanwhile, with General Watanachai already having been moved from his post as commander of the Third Army in September 2001, RTA chief Surayud was also replaced in a military reshuffle in October 2002.[35] By December, Task Force 399 was relieved of its drug suppression role and removed from the border area on the grounds that Myanmar regarded it with suspicion.[36] The Thaksin government decided to provide crossborder assistance with crop substitution in the Wa-controlled area of Yong Kha in Shan State.[37] These decisions removed key obstacles to Thaksin's dominance of Thailand's Myanmar policy and the improvement of bilateral ties.

Thanks to Thaksin, Myanmar's military leadership succeeded in building up unprecedented levels of confidence, both in the overall relationship and on the border. The general improvement in bilateral relations was best symbolised by the royal visit of Princess Maha Chakri Sirindhorn in March 2003, following visits first by the new commander-in-chief of the Army, General Somdhat Attanand and the commander of the Third Army

Region, Lieutenant General Udomchai Ongkhasingh in January as well as by Thaksin in February. The army commanders in their bilateral meeting reportedly reached agreement that military exercises in both countries would henceforth take place well away from the border and that each side would also warn the other of impending military exercises.[38]

Having offered without success to mediate between, on the one hand, the 'military alliance' of non-ceasefire groups, composed of the Karen National Union (KNU), the SSA, the Karenni National Progress Party, the Chin National Liberation Front and the Arakan Liberation Party and, on the other hand, the SPDC, Thailand in March publicly resolved to exert military pressure on the Karen National Union (KNU) and the SSA. Thai forces then pushed SSA-South camps closer towards the border and advised Yawd Serk to negotiate with the SPDC. (The difficulty is that the military regards SSA as a drug trafficking outfit that like the MTA is required to surrender unconditionally). Following the Depayin incident, Thailand attempted to continue its mediation role, this time between the regime and the wider regional and international society. To promote its interests in this way necessitated further confidence-building with SPDC leaders.

In January 2004, under Thai political pressure, the Office of the United Nations High Commissioner for Refugees (UNHCR) suspended its screening on the Thai side of the border of new asylum-seekers, raising questions about whether the Thai authorities would deport new arrivals as being illegal immigrants.[39] Bangkok also made attempts to relocate urban refugees to border camps, following various attempts to curtail the activities of the Burmese human-rights and pro-democracy movement. Thaksin has thus moved Thailand down precisely the path of cooperation that Myanmar had long favoured.[40] Speaking in April 2004, the Thai premier argued that at no time in recent years had there been 'better and closer relations'.[41] In effect, the Thaksin government had been at pains to repair the bilateral relationship to advance Thai security and business interests. Economic relations have developed well from the junta's perspective, with trade rising to US$2.26bn for the first 11 months of 2005, a rise of 17% over 2004, and generating a surplus of several hundred million dollars.[42] In April 2006, the two sides agreed to build another hydropower plant on the Thanlwin River, the US$6bn Ta Sang project. Overall, Myanmar's policy toward Thailand since 2001 has proved a considerable success as the SPDC has benefited substantially from changes in Thaksin's domestic policies and diplomacy. Meanwhile, ethnic-insurgent camps do remain along the border, and the potential for border crises to erupt again can not be discounted.

A more rocky phase since 2003

Despite significant improvements in ties with Thailand, Myanmar's overall relations with its ASEAN neighbours have become increasingly complicated since the Depayin incident of 30 May 2003.[43] There are at least two reasons for this.[44] First, ASEAN has come under increasing extramural pressure, not least from the US, to make Myanmar comply with international demands. Second, Myanmar's diplomatic responses, particularly its stalling tactics, have antagonised not only several member states whose newly installed leaderships are attempting to sharpen their own democratic and regional credentials, but also those who see the focus on Myanmar as a distraction from ASEAN's main challenges. In consequence, ASEAN solidarity has begun to wear thinner, leading to a growing propensity to criticise Myanamar's military government publicly. This has in turn led Myanmar to attempt to evade ASEAN censure, leading to new irritations.

Dealing with Depayin

ASEAN foreign ministers reacted to the Depayin incident by incorporating a paragraph on the situation in Myanmar into the Joint Communiqué released at the June 2003 AMM. Myanmar was urged to resume efforts towards national reconciliation and dialogue among all parties concerned to effect a peaceful transition to democracy. ASEAN foreign ministers also 'welcomed' Myanmar's assurances that ASSK's detention was temporary and looked forward to the early lifting of restrictions placed on her and other party members. Apparently informally, they even expressed a wish that ASSK should be released within a month of the AMM. Some were keen that ASEAN organise a ministerial troika to visit Yangon.[45]

To meet this unprecedented challenge from ASEAN, Win Aung and Deputy Foreign Minister Khin Maung Win travelled to Thailand and Malaysia, Singapore and Indonesia,[46] carrying both a personal letter from Than Shwe and photographs of ASSK to demonstrate her good health. The letter justified ASSK's protective custody on national security grounds insofar as the measure had been necessary to prevent the country from sliding towards anarchy and disintegration as a result of NLD attempts to create a mass movement that would stir up public demonstrations and unrest. The letter reportedly also suggested that ASSK had been attempting to lure ethnic-minority armed groups to join a planned uprising.[47] Apparently, it also sought understanding for the military government's inability to announce a deadline for ASSK's release. Meanwhile, Khin Nyunt complained that applying pressure and imposing sanctions amounted to the 'breaching of international laws and bullying of Myanmar'.[48]

Given the international repercussions of the incident, the SPDC's post-Depayin stance on ASSK in particular was found wanting by other ASEAN leaders. It even led Malaysia's ex-premier Dr Mahathir Mohamed to suggest that Myanmar might have to be expelled from ASEAN as 'a last resort' if Yangon failed to release ASSK. Myanmar could easily dismiss such a threat, as there was no legal basis for such a measure,[49] and the suggestion met with reservations in other ASEAN capitals. Thaksin offered to mediate between the SPDC and the wider regional and international society, and proposed a meeting bringing together all concerned countries to discuss a 'road map toward democracy'.[50] But Myanmar's position within ASEAN remained difficult as Indonesia, then-chair of ASEAN's Standing Committee, saw dealing with the fallout of the Depayin incident as an important question of leadership, not least because Jakarta was hosting the ASEM Foreign Ministers' Meeting and the Asia–Africa Sub-Regional Organisation Conference (AASROC) in Bandung in late July and the ASEAN Summit in October 2003. Jakarta was above all concerned that developments in Myanmar might derail the ASEAN Summit.

Myanmar's leadership faced a serious foreign-policy dilemma: how to politically sideline ASSK in accordance with its domestic political-security imperative, while satisfying the demands of fellow ASEAN countries for her release? In the event, the regime politely hinted at pressure being an imperfect instrument of policy, while indicating a preparedness to meet some of ASEAN's key concerns. U Win Aung pointedly asked why Myanmar should be pushed back into the shell from which it had emerged, suggesting that ASEAN had a continued interest in continued engagement.[51] Nonetheless, after meeting his Indonesian counterpart, Dr Hassan Wirajuda, on the sidelines of the AASROC event in Bandung, U Win Aung implied that the case would be solved by the time of the ASEAN Summit in October.[52] Meanwhile, he rejected the idea of an ASEAN Troika visiting Yangon.

Having initially reacted cautiously to Thailand's 'road map' proposal and the idea of an international forum to discuss Myanmar, U Win Aung visited Bangkok in early August to learn more from Sathirathai about the plan.[53] However, the specifics of Thailand's road map proved unacceptable to the SPDC, as it identified the release of ASSK and other NLD leaders as a first step, to be followed by confidence-building between the government and the opposition, the drafting and adoption of a new constitution and, ultimately, the organisation of free elections.[54] Khin Nyunt, therefore, announced the SPDC's own road map at the end of August 2003. This outlined seven steps to a 'disciplined flourishing democracy', starting with the reconvening of the NC, adjourned since 1996, and then proceeding with the drafting of a new constitution, its adoption by national referendum, the holding of free and fair elections for *Pyithu Hluttaw* (legislative bodies) according to the new constitution, the convening of these *Hluttaw*, and the building of a modern, developed and democratic nation by newly elected state leaders.[55]

Because Yangon's road map made no mention of ASSK and failed to clarify whether Myanmar would comply with Indonesia's demand to release ASSK before the ASEAN Summit, it did not enjoy unequivocal support within ASEAN.[56] Indeed, within days of Hassan Wirajuda reiterating this central expectation in early September, Indonesian President Megawati Sukarnoputri sent a special envoy to secure ASSK's release. In the event, the SPDC twice received the envoy, Ali Alatas, who had played a pivotal role in Myanmar's accession to ASEAN in 1997, but offered no indication as to the future status of ASSK, who was at the time recuperating in hospital from unexpected surgery.[57] Myanmar's leadership similarly received Sathirathai, in his capacity as Thaksin's special envoy, and again made no concessions. Once discharged from hospital, however, ASSK was moved to her home, which elicited a positive response from Indonesia and Thailand during the informal ASEAN Foreign Ministers' Meeting on the sidelines of the UN General Assembly in September. With guarded praise under his belt for both the seven-point road map and the apparent termination of ASSK's detention, Khin Nyunt attended the ASEAN Summit in Bali. Myanmar's top diplomats had read the situation well. Indonesia badly wanted the summit and the media to focus on the idea of the ASEAN Community and the ASEAN Security Community in particular, while Thaksin was keen to promote Bangkok's improving ties with Myanmar. At the time, other ASEAN members had no interest in rocking the boat. Consequently, the ASEAN Summit declared that the road map constituted 'a pragmatic approach and deserves understanding and support'. The summit's statement even stressed that sanctions would not help to promote the peace and stability essential for democracy to take root. Significantly, however, Myanmar failed to acknowledge or appreciate that despite this positive outcome there was no change in ASEAN's position on the early lifting of restrictions imposed on ASSK. As ASEAN diplomats saw it, the summit statement reflected in the first instance the understanding that Khin Nyunt would need some time to put the road map into action.

In November 2003, Hassan Wirajuda unexpectedly asked for a timetable of the road map to be made public.[58] The Myanmar government declined to provide this information, deciding instead to pursue the Thai idea subsequently dubbed the 'Bangkok Process', not only to explain the road map to 'like-minded' countries,[59] but also to announce the reconvening in 2004 of the NC, which had been suspended since 1996. With representatives of the 'national races' and political parties invited to the NC, the NLD was also offered the opportunity to rejoin the process. The NLD made its participation dependent on the release of ASSK and U Tin Oo. However, prior to the NC's re-launch in May 2004, U Win Aung had more than once seemingly indicated that ASSK might be freed before proceedings resumed,[60] but the top leadership ultimately decided against it. The SPDC also decided against participating in a second round of the Bangkok Process, scheduled for late April 2004, claiming that it was preparing for the upcoming NC. Thailand nonetheless remained one of Myanmar's major supporters and defenders within ASEAN, advocating the view that ASEAN should help reduce international pressure on Yangon. As a grouping, however, ASEAN used the 2004 AMM to restate indirectly its formal position adopted the previous year. Myanmar had embarked on the NC in full conformity with its political-security imperative, but continued to defy ASEAN's collective call for the release of ASSK.

While the ASEAN Summit Statement of 2003 had been considerably more positive than the outcome of the AMM the previous June, the 2004 ASEAN Summit Statement made no reference at all to Myanmar.[61] The main reason was that Thaksin had issued an advance warning to other heads of government that he intended to walk out of the summit meeting if the insurgency in southern Thailand, particularly the Tak Bai incident, were raised by them.[62] Thaksin's stance impacted on how ASEAN leaders could address the lack of political progress in Myanmar with new Prime Minister Soe Win in that to prevent a double standard from being applied, ASEAN could comment on neither the developments in Thailand nor those in Myanmar. Yangon in fact gained some credibility because the regime released more than 9,000 prisoners in the days leading up to the summit. However, by renewing ASSK's detention while the summit was underway, the SPDC prompted an outcry from some ASEAN members. Indeed, if the regime believed that ASEAN's failure to censure Myanmar implied an early diplomatic victory, it was essentially mistaken.

Chairmanship of the ASEAN Standing Committee in 2005

As spring 2005 approached, the implementation of the road map and the release of ASSK on the one hand, and the question of Myanmar's ASEAN chairmanship in 2006–07 on the other, ultimately became inextricably linked. This linkage had been explicitly established for several months by regional parliamentarians, the media and civil-society groups. But ASEAN governments had until then chosen not to acknowledge it. This changed when, in February 2005, Philippine President Gloria Macapagal-Arroyo raised Myanmar-related issues during a visit by Soe Win. Thereafter Badawi suggested that the SPDC needed to make 'visible progress' with its road map before Myanmar could assume the ASEAN chair. Speaking of a need for 'hard messages', remarks by Singapore Foreign Minister George Yeo to parliament in March 2005 underlined unease within ASEAN about Myanmar chairing the association. By the end of March Indonesia had also qualitatively shifted its position by suggesting that, given the lack of tangible progress on the road map, Yangon should sort out its domestic problems before assuming chairmanship of ASEAN. Visiting Yangon in late March, Singapore Prime Minister Lee Hsien Loong conveyed this message in person.

In April 2005, therefore, at the time of the ASEAN Foreign Ministers' Retreat organised on Cebu in the Philippines, Myanmar faced its most significant ASEAN-related decision since joining the Association. At stake was whether Yangon should assume the ASEAN chairmanship in the face of exhortations to give up the opportunity. There were effectively three options. The first was to assume the chair and to host both the November 2006 ASEAN Summit (which apart from the ASEAN-10 was to involve China, Japan, South Korea as well as India, New Zealand and possibly Australia) as well as the ministerial meetings the following July (the AMM, the Post-Ministerial Conference [PMC] meetings with the ASEAN Dialogue Partners and the ARF). This option carried considerable risk as it would probably exacerbate divisions within ASEAN, particularly if the US were to make good on its threat to refuse to send a senior official to the ASEAN PMC and ARF meetings scheduled for 2007 and even to suspend funds for regional development projects. Another factor was that many of Myanmar's personnel knowledgeable about ASEAN had lost their political footing with the disbandment of Khin Nyunt's MI in October 2004. The second was for Myanmar to ask to organise the summit meetings, but to leave the organisation of the 2007 ministerial meetings to the Philippines. Under this scenario Myanmar would still win considerable prestige because the summit ranked above the ministerial meetings. However, as Yangon understood, this sort of 'cherry-picking' was never going to be acceptable in the eyes of other ASEAN members. The third was to request that Myanmar should at least temporarily forego its chairmanship. Though the decision whether to proceed with the chairmanship was left in Myanmar's hands at the Cebu Retreat, members made clear that in reaching its decision, the junta should act in ASEAN's interests.

This is precisely what Myanmar did at the July 2005 ASEAN Foreign Ministers' Meeting in Vientiane. According to the ASEAN Joint Statement:

'Myanmar had decided to relinquish its turn to be the Chair of ASEAN in 2006 because it would want to focus its attention on the ongoing national reconciliation and democratization process'.[63] Although the final decision on the issue is considered to have been reached only shortly before the AMM, Myanmar had communicated a provisional decision to China and some ASEAN countries even before the Cebu Retreat.[64] Nevertheless, to avoid the impression that Myanmar was reacting to external pressure rather than simply exercising its own sovereign decision, Yangon took its time in putting an end to the uncertainty that prevailed on the chairmanship issue between April and July.

By temporarily surrendering the chairmanship, Yangon succeeded in defusing the awkward situation in which it had put fellow members. As Yeo put it: 'We appreciate their factoring in of ASEAN and we believe that by decoupling the Chairmanship of ASEAN from their domestic politics, this is good for their own domestic politics and is also good for ASEAN'.[65] Notably, ASEAN states expressed their intention not to prevent Myanmar from assuming the ASEAN chairmanship whenever the SPDC felt it was ready for it. The regime has already signalled, however, that it does not want to assume the chairmanship even in 2007–08.

In September 2005, the publication of the Havel–Tutu report, prepared by an international law firm,[66] almost immediately led the ASEAN Interparliamentary Myanmar Caucus (AIPMC) to also favour placing Myanmar on the UNSC agenda and express support for United Nations Secretary-General (UNSG) Kofi Annan to lead a coordinated international campaign to pressure the SPDC into accepting genuine democratic reforms.[67] In contrast, ASEAN's position remained unchanged although many of its member states hoped to see the regime make faster progress in implementing its road map. Yet when visiting Myanmar in October, Syed Hamid, Malaysia's foreign minister and chair of the ASEAN Standing Committee, was reportedly informed by Than Shwe, Soe Win and Nyan Win that Myanmar remained cautious about adopting democracy because the government wanted to avoid chaos and a descent into Iraq-style unrest.[68] Kuala Lumpur intimated that Myanmar would again not feature on the formal agenda of the December 2005 ASEAN Summit.

However, following US complaints at the November Asia Pacific Economic Cooperation (APEC) Leaders' Meeting about Myanmar's neighbours not putting sufficient pressure on Myanmar, Arroyo indicated support for efforts to have the UNSC discuss Myanmar.[69] As Manila was at this time a non-permanent UNSC member, the US could argue that it had sufficient support to place Myanmar on the UNSC agenda.[70] The

Philippines' support constituted an extraordinary diplomatic move by one ASEAN state against another, starkly illustrating the limits of ASEAN's collective foreign policy and its status as a diplomatic community. Because UNSC members only agreed to a briefing during informal deliberations, however, Manila was not obliged to cast its vote and thereby completely shatter ASEAN's facade.

Startled by this development, Myanmar's military regime equally found little cheer in featuring prominently in discussions among foreign ministers in the lead-up to the ASEAN Summit in Kuala Lumpur in December 2005. Syed Hamid vented ASEAN's frustration with the SPDC publicly, arguing that all member states were impatient and uncomfortable with the latter's progress towards democracy. Suggesting, moreover, that Myanmar should be more responsive to the international community's wishes, he raised the idea of an ASEAN delegation visiting Yangon to ascertain progress in implementing the road map. Badawi also suggested that ASEAN could no longer defend the SPDC if it remained unclear about the situation in Myanmar. On this basis, the SPDC perfunctorily agreed in principle only to a visit by Syed Hamid as ASEAN chair. The chair's Summit Statement welcomed this decision, also calling for the release of those placed under detention.[71]

Pointing to its preoccupation with the relocation of government offices to the new administrative capital Naypyidaw, 400 km north of Yangon, the SPDC declined to receive Syed Hamid until March 2006. The real reason for this procrastination was his request for a meeting with ASSK, to which the regime was not prepared to accede, even though or because the Malaysian foreign minister had reportedly made it a prerequisite for future ASEAN solidarity.[72] While Syed Hamid's visit was postponed in the face of increasingly blunt criticisms by several ASEAN members, Myanmar received first Indonesian President Dr Susilo Bambang Yodhoyono and then the Indian President, Dr A.P.J. Abdul Kalam. Not burdened by requests for a meeting with ASSK, Yodhoyono's introductory visit had a critical edge nonetheless, in that Indonesia suggested that Myanmar should learn from Indonesia's political transition towards democracy, accept the idea of regional monitors and engage in constant communication with ASEAN and the international community. Both sides, moreover, exchanged views on their expectations regarding the implementation of Myanmar's road map, though these have not been made public to hide any hint of the SPDC reacting to external pressure.[73] When it was finally arranged, the visit by Malaysia's foreign minister proved only a partial success for ASEAN, encapsulated by Syed Hamid's assessment that his inability to speak to every stakeholder, meaning ASSK and the NLD, and even Than Shwe, made it 'incomplete'.[74]

Nevertheless, at the ASEAN Foreign Ministers' Retreat in Ubud, Bali, in April 2006 to which Malaysia's foreign minister reported as ASC chair, the public criticisms of Myanmar did not go beyond those already levelled at Myanmar the previous December, regardless of suggestions in advance of the meeting that there would be some tough talk.

Whither Myanmar–ASEAN relations?

Myanmar's military-led government is by and large confident that, given the grouping's emphasis on non-interference and its interest in not seeing extra-regional countries impose a political solution on a member state, ASEAN will continue providing Yangon with diplomatic-political support. The underlying analysis is broadly accurate. ASEAN is not about to abandon its existing institutional and normative framework, although members are increasingly happy to practice what the Association calls 'enhanced interaction', and in December 2005 agreed to establish an Eminent Persons Group to examine and provide practical recommenda-tions on the directions for ASEAN and the nature of the ASEAN Charter that is capable of meeting the needs of the ASEAN Community. It has at no point as a grouping viewed Myanmar as an issue for the UNSC. Syed Hamid unambiguously agreed with China and Russia that Myanmar does not pose a regional security concern.[75] Moreover, ASEAN has not argued that the regime's road map is flawed per se. Whereas in 2003 (before the reconvening of the NC), ASEAN foreign ministers urged Myanmar to resume efforts aimed at national reconciliation and dialogue among all parties concerned, the 2005 Summit Statement instead offered encour-agement to Myanmar to expedite the implementation of its road map. Malaysia's request that the SPDC clarify Myanmar's progress in moving forward with its own road map amounted to a plea for Yangon to demon-strate sufficient political commitment to avoid burdening ASEAN's external relations and to make certain that extra-regional actors do not become any more deeply involved.

The SPDC may also think that it has two trump cards that will ensure continued ASEAN support, and if necessary, enable it to cope with added pressure. The first is that Myanmar was admitted to ASEAN in part to lessen its dependence on China. That rationale has retained its salience. The second is that Myanmar has the option in the last resort of leaving ASEAN. Both calculations impose a constraint on the association. Already, before the 2005 AMM in Vientiane, officials in some member states were concerned that if ASEAN put too much pressure on Myanmar, the latter might contemplate leaving the association. If that were to happen, ASEAN could no longer claim to represent Southeast Asia as a whole. Such a step could damage ASEAN more than Myanmar, not least because ASEAN would have to pay a serious diplomatic price to see Myanmar rejoin the association, unless there was significant prior political change in the country.

Yet Myanmar's leaders appreciate that they cannot hope to receive as much support from ASEAN in future as they have done in the past. Increasingly, their foreign policy presents most ASEAN countries with a serious dilemma. On the one hand, its members insist that Myanmar is not the main dimension in their relationship with the West. On the other, these states find themselves under mounting international pressure to respond more vigorously to developments in Myanmar. The decision by US Secretary of State Condoleezza Rice not to attend the 2005 ASEAN PMC and ARF meetings due to a 'scheduling conflict' was widely interpreted as an expression of US dissatisfaction with ASEAN's handling of the Myanmar issue. Conversely, Indonesia and ASEAN saw their recent diplomatic efforts towards Myanmar applauded by the Secretary of State. Unsurprisingly, exasperated ASEAN governments ask pointed questions about why they should offer Myanmar diplomatic support if the SPDC continues to implement unswervingly the political-security imperative even at the cost of ASEAN's collective reputation. The allegedly sudden and unexpected move of the administrative capital to Naypyidaw has been represented by ASEAN governments as a vivid demonstration of the regime's lack of regard for other members. ASEAN leaders also appreciate that the association or its members do not have any substantial sway over the SPDC. The military did eventually accommodate Indonesia's summit-related concerns in 2003 to some extent, but its decision in 2006 to delay the ASEAN Standing Committee chairman's visit and its outcome again clearly demonstrate the limits of ASEAN's influence. With individual members formulating their positions towards Myanmar not merely with reference to ASEAN but in the wider context of their foreign-policy concerns and considerations, a united ASEAN stance on Myanmar cannot be taken for granted.

Indonesia, with its new democratic identity, its post-crisis foreign-policy ambitions, and the importance it attaches to the strengthening of ASEAN, certainly looks at Myanmar differently than it did in the 1990s, as indicated by Hassan Wirajuda's comment in January 2006 that Myanmar was 'disturbing the balance' of ASEAN.[76] Singapore, which benefits from a strategic partnership with Washington, has on more than one occasion suggested that ASEAN might need to take hard decisions on Myanmar, but is keen to see Myanmar preserve its independent foreign policy. Thaksin's efforts to promote confidence-building with the regime to allow it to mediate between Myanmar and its detractors have proved controversial both within Thailand and in the United States, and it remains to be seen how relations between Bangkok and Naypyidaw will evolve once Thailand's political crisis of early 2006 has been resolved. The Philippines was already once prepared to see Myanmar discussed by the UNSC. In contrast, Laos, Vietnam and Cambodia have remained broadly supportive of the regime.

Significantly, Myanmar has made it very clear that it does not like and will not respond to public pressure from the association. Interestingly, Myanmar was the only country absent from the first-ever formal meeting of ASEAN defence ministers in May 2006. Although these developments may not be directly connected, it is clear that there is more potential for Myanmar to become increasingly disenchanted with ASEAN, as the pressure the grouping puts on the SPDC grows. ASEAN's significance in Myanmar's foreign policy has already declined, as more emphasis has been put by the regime on developing bilateral relations with its immediate neighbours in the first instance.

Conclusion

Myanmar joined ASEAN because it saw this step as being in its economic and political-strategic interests. The direct economic gains of membership have proved more elusive than anticipated, but ASEAN has offered Myanmar important political returns. The key achievement at the bilateral level, with implications for the overall Myanmar–ASEAN relationship, has been the improvement of ties with Thailand. Though Yangon initially did not expect a serious challenge from ASEAN on the SPDC's political-security imperative, the military leadership has found that its domestic practices, particularly the treatment of ASSK since 2003, have become an issue in relations with the grouping. This has further diminished the returns of ASEAN membership, which can no longer be taken completely for granted. However, in the face of persistent pressure from the United States, even though the grouping may not want to go any further than calling on Yangon to expedite democratisation and to release political detainees, the SPDC could find that ASEAN solidarity is in increasingly short supply.

CHAPTER FOUR

Relations with the West and Japan

Dealing effectively with the United States, Europe and Japan has constituted a major challenge for Myanmar's military government. While these advanced industrialised countries could potentially play a major part in Myanmar's economic development, none of them do. Instead, all have chosen to exert political pressure on the regime. Though this pressure has increased over the years, the SLORC/SPDC has consistently prioritised its political-security imperative over better relations with the West and Japan. ASSK was twice released (in 1995 and 2002) with a view to improving political and economic ties, but these improvements failed to materialise because the regime has consistently rejected Western and Japanese calls to start a 'genuine' and inclusive national dialogue, and not hesitated to defy other political demands. Since the Depayin incident, Myanmar and the US, in particular, have been firmly locked in a battle of wills, although relations with the EU and Japan have also deteriorated. For Washington, 'Burma' seems increasingly to be a Southeast Asian case for the US's global promotion of freedom. Conversely, for the SPDC, the US now presents the major foreign-policy challenge.

Policy towards Myanmar

The United States, Europe and Japan have developed somewhat different attitudes and policies towards the military regime. This is illustrated by the diverse ways in which they refer to the country. For Washington, Myanmar remains 'Burma'; for the Europeans, when formulating their collective or common policy, Myanmar is 'Burma/Myanmar'; and for Tokyo, Myanmar is

'Myanmar'. More importantly, differences have extended to the key political demands made of Yangon. In the 1990s, the United States regularly impressed on the military government the need to recognise and honour the results of the 1990 elections with an attendant transfer of power to a civilian government. It has continued to call for a transition to democratic rule and greater respect for human rights,[1] co-sponsoring the annual resolutions concerning Myanmar at the UN General Assembly and the UNCHR. For a brief period, from 2002–03, the US offered to look seriously at measures to support constructive political change in Myanmar. Following the Depayin incident, however, the State Department again focused uncompromisingly on the 'restoration of democracy'. To this end Bush signed the Burmese Freedom and Democracy Act in July 2003.[2] The US has pursued as immediate objectives the release of ASSK and all political prisoners, and a genuine dialogue on democratic political reform, including the re-opening of all NLD party offices.

By contrast, the European position throughout has effectively been that though there should be greater respect for human rights and a transition to democracy and civilian rule, new elections would be acceptable. Japan has called on the regime to progress towards democratisation and to improve the human-rights situation. Both the West and Japan have called for the release of ASSK. Differences in basic positions and goals have been highlighted by differences in the purpose and use of sanctions. US sanctions have in practice primarily aimed to isolate Myanmar politically and to cripple it economically in order either to force the regime to stand aside or to create conditions that would lead to its overthrow; European sanctions have aimed to weaken, punish and disgrace the military leadership and to spur a change in its domestic practices; meanwhile, Japan has in effect opted for a form of strongly conditional engagement that has stopped Tokyo from providing Official Development Assistance (ODA) to prompt changes in the regime's behaviour. To illustrate this point: Washington has, since the late 1980s, blocked loans by the IMF, World Bank and Asian Development Bank (ADB) (considered by the US to be the single most important form of pressure on Myanmar), suspended economic aid, withdrawn trade privileges, instituted an arms embargo, downgraded representation in Yangon to chargé-d'affaires level and imposed visa restrictions on senior leaders and their families. President Bill Clinton banned new US investments. President George W. Bush imposed a total ban on the import of Myanmar products as well as the export of financial services to Myanmar by US citizens, while also introducing a targeted asset freeze and extending existing visa restrictions.

Though continuously amended, European sanctions remain less severe than those of Washington. They have included a stop to: the exchange of military attachés; the sale, supply, transfer or export of arms and related material of all types; the financing or financial assistance related to military activities; and the freezing of funds. Non-humanitarian aid and development programmes have been suspended, unless in support of human rights and democracy, poverty alleviation, or health and basic education when provided by NGOs. Visa restrictions for key representatives of the military regime and their families have been imposed, along with a suspension of high-level governmental visits to Myanmar. Separately, in 1997 Myanmar saw its privileges based on the Generalised System of Preferences withdrawn due to European concerns about forced labour.[3] Since then, the export of equipment that might be used in domestic repression has been prohibited, the existing travel ban has been expanded to include transit visas, and persons affected by the visa ban have been listed publicly and had EU-based assets frozen. In contrast, Japan has only suspended economic cooperation and has even been prepared to re-consider and re-start on a case-by-case basis suspended development projects that would directly benefit the people of Myanmar by addressing their basic human needs. That policy was temporarily revisited only after Depayin.[4]

The economic impact of Western sanctions on Myanmar should not be underestimated, though even under normal circumstances Yangon might not qualify for assistance without serious changes to its economic policies. Myanmar is the only Southeast Asian country unable to draw on official development assistance from international financial institutions (IFI). This applies even when, as in the case of the multilateral GMS Programme, Myanmar's partners receive funds from the ADB for projects that include Myanmar. US trade sanctions imposed after 30 May 2003 have wiped out approximately US\$350m in exports to the US, and led to serious job losses in Myanmar's textile industry.[5] In 2004, Myanmar's exports to the European Union states and Japan amount to €402m and €131m respectively.

Conditions for reviewing sanctions have also differed. The US government has advised that its sanctions will be 'maintained until there is significant progress toward political transition and genuine respect for human rights or until a democratically elected government in Burma requests that they be lifted.'[6] The EU's 'Common Position' allows for a suspension of restrictive measures and a gradual resumption of cooperation if there is a substantial improvement in the overall political situation. Japan's position is apparently that any future comprehensive renewal of aid depends on democratisation and, in particular, the release of ASSK, but also on her tacit approval.

Regarding Myanmar's national reconciliation process and the ongoing NC, policy convergence among the US, EU and Japan is again more limited than is first apparent. The US has demanded the immediate and unconditional release of ASSK and all political prisoners, the re-opening of all NLD party offices and the start of a meaningful dialogue leading to genuine national reconciliation and the establishment of constitutional democracy. It regards the NC as lacking domestic and international credibility and legitimacy: in short it is a 'sham'. The EU has worried that prospects for real and inclusive national reconciliation remain poor given the SPDC's absolute control over the NC and the failure to reach agreement between ASSK and the SPDC leadership on NLD participation. The European Commission has called on the SPDC to ensure that the NLD and all ethnic nationality groups may participate in NC deliberations. Meanwhile, Tokyo has argued that the NC could be a significant step towards democratisation, while also expressing concern that the NC started without all the relevant parties being involved. This raises questions as to whether the NC would be able to hold 'substantively meaningful' discussions. Tokyo has called on Yangon to make further efforts in this respect. Japan has also voiced strongly its hopes that Myanmar will expedite democratisation, including ASSK's release. Given these different approaches, it is unsurprising that Myanmar's foreign policy towards the United States, Europe and Japan has also diverged. Among the three Western power centres, most attention has inevitably focused on the United States, the greatest perceived threat to Myanmar's security, and Japan, the most muted critic of the three.

Myanmar's foreign policy towards the United States

Myanmar's foreign policy towards the United States has been largely reactive. This reflects the regime's understanding that while it wishes to resist US pressure, it has very little if any leverage to alter the dynamics and tone of the bilateral relationship, short of relinquishing power. Yet giving in to Washington's central demand for regime transition is unacceptable to the military-led government. The SPDC sees itself as the only institution able to guarantee national unity and stability in the longer term given the difficult relations between the Burman majority and the ethnic-minority groups as well as the perceived disastrous historical experience of Burmese democratic politics which, in the view of the military, saw politicians indulge in personally motivated struggles and internecine squabbling at the expense of national interests. In any case, Washington's demands are considered as utterly unwarranted interference. As the former regime spokesman Hla Min put it, 'As a sovereign independent country we do not like to be pushed around.'[7] The SPDC effectively sees US sanctions and its support for the NLD and ASSK and other pro-democracy activists as a form of low-intensity warfare. Yet it appreciates the enormous disparity in power between the two countries. While it feels it should and must resist US government demands for the national good, the military leadership thus remains keen neither to open itself up to full confrontation nor to burn all bridges. Accordingly, Myanmar's foreign policy towards Washington combines elements of defiance over the SPDC's priorities for regime survival, national unity and stability with cooperative behaviour in multilateral and bilateral settings. The SPDC has, for instance, taken action in response to US concerns over political reconciliation when dealing with the United Nations, as illustrated by its early record of cooperation with the UN Special Envoy Ambassador Razali Ismail. The same point can be made about human rights and the record of cooperation initially established with UN Special Rapporteur for Human Rights, Professor Sergio Pinheiro. Myanmar indirectly for a while also addressed some of America's concerns in relation to forced labour when dealing with the ILO. Most of this cooperation was extended in the last years preceding Khin Nyunt's removal in 2004. Myanmar also co-signed the US–ASEAN Declaration on Cooperation Against Terrorism in August 2002. It has also ratified relevant UN conventions. In terms of bilateral cooperation, the regime shared intelligence with the US and quietly opened its airspace for US military flights to the Middle East.[8] Overall, as Washington admitted in early 2004, the SPDC has provided 'solid cooperation' on counter-terrorism issues.[9] Myanmar has also cooperated on the full accounting of missing US servicemen from the Second World War and, since 1993, on the annual joint poppy-yield survey. Cooperation on counter-narcotics with the Drug Enforcement Administration has not been matched by cooperation on money laundering, though.

However, the SPDC leadership has found Washington even more unyielding than it considers itself justifiably to have been. In effect, whatever Myanmar has done to improve its international standing and relations with the West, the American government has maintained the pressure by confronting the military government and also urging the European Union, Japan and ASEAN to tighten their respective Myanmar policies. US administrations have used international and regional organisations – such as the UN, particularly the UNGA and the UNCHR, the ILO and the ARF – to embarrass and criticise Myanmar. Significantly, releasing ASSK from house arrest has not helped. The military twice did so, partially in the hope that such a step would help to improve relations with Washington. Yet instead of seeing Washington's political pressure weaken, or even a review of the utility of sanctions, on both occasions the SLORC/SPDC found the US government only offering a short-lived acclamation.

Following her initial release in July 1995, Washington remarked positively on the space granted to ASSK to pursue her political activities, but over the next two years severely criticised the junta's reluctance to meet directly with her. With the assumption of Madeleine Albright, previously US ambassador to the UN, to the post of secretary of state in January 1997, the relationship had nowhere to go, such was Albright's repugnance towards the regime and the vehemence of her support for ASSK. Indeed, the military government at the time accused the US embassy in Yangon of orchestrating ASSK's political challenge. Notably, when the military responded angrily to the NLD's calculated move in August 1998 to form the Committee Representing the People's Parliament on the basis of the 1990 election, a move considered to be an attempt to create a parallel government, the US government deplored the SPDC's reaction to reject a 'historic opportunity'.

The military leadership, particularly Khin Nyunt, nevertheless hoped for a relaxation in bilateral ties and international recognition after embarking on a more sustained effort from 2000 to promote national reconciliation, which led to the second release from house arrest of ASSK in May 2002.[10] But Yangon again found Washington largely unimpressed. The US government commented favourably on SPDC confidence-building measures in advance of ASSK's release, particularly Yangon's cooperation with the UN and the ICRC. It also acknowledged that ASSK's release involved a 'change from conditions in her pre-detention days' as she could travel freely throughout Myanmar.[11] The furthest Washington was prepared to go in response, however, was to allow IFI fact-finding and technical assistance.[12] The State Department suggested that should there be significant progress towards democracy and greater respect for human rights, the US would look seriously at measures to support such a constructive process. In the event, the State Department expressed disappointment that ASSK was unable to talk to the regime's core leadership and the SPDC's reluctance to open a dialogue with her on constitutional issues. This suggests that Yangon insufficiently understood the depth of Washington's reluctance to accept the political-security imperative of the *Tatmadaw*. For the State Department, questions about the SPDC's overall commitment to political transition certainly remained, and it warned: 'Absent progress, we will be forced to consider, in conjunction with the international community, additional sanctions and or other measures'.[13] When ASSK was placed under 'protective custody' in 2003, US encouragement immediately gave way to vilification, as Secretary of State Colin L. Powell made '[t]hugs representing the thugs in power' responsible for the Depayin incident.[14] From the point of view of Myanmar's military leadership, then, what had been a contentious bid to place relations with the West on a new footing ultimately produced no tangible or lasting concrete foreign-policy gains.

Significantly, the SPDC had hoped that the US would at least take Myanmar off the list of countries considered to be major drug-producing states, which would allow Yangon to receive counter-narcotics assistance from Washington. Although Washington had financially supported counter-narcotics operations in Myanmar from 1974 to 1988, the US had since not certified Myanmar as a country sufficiently cooperating on drug elimination, leaving Yangon to provide funds and personnel to eradicate poppy cultivation in areas held by ethnic groups. Myanmar has claimed that it has kept at least US$45bn worth of heroin off US streets.[15] Without such certification, the country is by law ineligible for US foreign assistance except narcotics control aid and humanitarian aid, and Washington must veto proposed IFI loans to Myanmar. Yangon even hired DCI Associates, a lobbying firm with alleged ties to the Bush family,[16] to lobby for certification for its cooperation. In the event, in 2003 the US government judged that Myanmar had 'failed demonstrably' to make substantial efforts to cooperate on narcotics matters even though by that year Myanmar was estimated to have cut opium production to roughly one fourth, 630 tonnes, of the 1996 figure of 2560 tonnes. The following year, estimated production decreased further to 484 tonnes, a decline of 81% since 1996.[17] Certification was denied on the grounds of Myanmar's soaring production of methamphetamines and their flow mainly into Thailand, and the limited and belated law enforcement actions by the military junta in respect of the UWSA. However, Myanmar does not produce precursors for synthetic drugs. Nor, evidently, does it control the ethnic-minority ceasefire groups, particularly the UWSA.

Observers of US policy towards Myanmar argue that Washington's hardening stand has resulted largely from the Bush administration giving in to Congressional demands, not least from Senator Mitch McConnell, who became the Republican whip in November 2002 and chairs the Subcommittee on State, Foreign Operations, and Related Programs of the US Senate Committee on Appropriations.[18] McConnell has for years demanded the release of ASSK, advocated regime change and expressed doubts about the integrity of the counter-narcotics effort. He has described Myanmar as a 'clear and present danger to the people of Burma and the entire region'.[19] He has also called for targeted US and UNSC sanctions.[20] There has also been intense lobbying in Washington by Burmese anti-regime and human rights activists.

Since 2002 there has been a conspicuous increase in ever more specific and specified US foreign-policy objectives towards Myanmar. Whereas during the two Clinton administrations, US policy goals towards Myanmar were broadly grouped under the categories of democracy, human rights and counter-narcotics, the Bush administration had by the end of its first term identified two immediate US policy objectives and 11 overall objectives.[21] The immediate objectives focused on: the release of NLD leaders ASSK, U Tin Oo and other members, the release of all other political prisoners and the re-opening of all NLD offices; and the start of a genuine dialogue on democracy and political reform.[22] The 11 overall objectives focus on: establishing constitutional democracy; respect for human rights and religious freedom; the repatriation of refugees with monitoring by the UNHCR; the return home of internally displaced persons; cooperation in fighting terrorism; regional stability; the full accounting of missing US serviceman; the combatting of HIV/AIDS; the elimination of people-trafficking; ending forced labour; and increased cooperation in eradicating the production and trafficking of illicit drugs.

The SPDC has spoken out strongly against Washington's support for ASSK and US government allegations of human-rights violations have routinely been rejected as one-sided and unbalanced, 'riddled with errors' and containing assertions 'almost none of which are backed up with evidence or with responsible sources'.[23] On occasion Yangon may have had a valid point in dismissing US assertions. For instance, Washington's claim that ASSK had gone on hunger strike in August 2003 – made just after Khin Nyunt's announcement of the seven-point road map – was subsequently exposed as untrue by the ICRC.[24] The military government has emphasised that given Myanmar's overall political situation it does not have the luxury of focusing its decisions on the 'interests of just one person' (ASSK). Stubbornly defending its record in dealing with the ethnic-minority ceasefire groups, it has expressed disappointment at the failure of the US government to acknowledge properly the regime's road map for democracy,[25] and repeatedly argued that 'sanctions delay or even derail the proper evolution to a democracy'. The broadening of US foreign-policy objectives under President Bush has reinforced the SPDC's view that Myanmar constitutes an easy target which can be attacked by US policy-makers at little or no cost to Washington. It has also made the regime attentive to other areas of possible controversy.

Nuclear and missile concerns

While re-affirming the political-security imperative, the SPDC has understood the possible danger of being seen as a threat to regional security. This perhaps became obvious in the context of concerns in 2002 about Myanmar potentially purchasing a nuclear reactor from Russia and subsequent rumours that there was a nuclear and missile link between Myanmar and North Korea. The situation first arose in 2001 when Myanmar and Russia negotiated a draft agreement for the sale of a 10-megawatt nuclear-research reactor to Yangon. An apparent pet project of Minister of Science U Thaung,[26] the reactor was, it seems, intended for medical purposes and possibly nuclear power generation, although status and prestige may have been additional drivers.[27] At the time, Deputy Foreign Minister Khin Maung Win said that under the Non-Proliferation Treaty, which Myanmar signed in 1992, it had the right to pursue 'the peaceful use and application of nuclear technology'. Myanmar also maintains a comprehensive safeguards agreement with the IAEA and is, moreover, a signatory of the 1995 Treaty of Bangkok, the Treaty on the Southeast Asia Nuclear Weapons Free Zone. Responding to proliferation concerns in the context of the 'global war on terror', Myanmar vigorously denied reports that two Pakistani nuclear scientists with alleged ties to al-Qaeda had come to Myanmar to assist with the work on the research reactor.

In the event, negotiations on the sale of the reactor ended in 2002, apparently owing to Yangon's lack of funds. Before long, however, new reports surfaced, this time establishing a supposed nuclear link between North Korea and Myanmar.[28] Responding to Congressional fears that Pyongyang might transfer to Myanmar both nuclear technology and *Scud* surface-to-surface missiles, then-US Deputy Assistant Secretary of State Matthew Daley met U Tin Win, minister in the prime minister's office, in New York in October 2003 to discuss the issue.[29] Despite Myanmar having reassured Washington on the matter, US expressions of concern re-surfaced in early 2004. In February 2004 the Myanmar government's information committee slammed 'irresponsible and unprofessional remarks' by an aide for US Senator Richard Lugar, who had suggested that North Korea might be providing nuclear technology to Myanmar.[30] In March 2004, the SPDC again maintained that it had 'no desire, nor any intention, of developing nuclear weapons, or other weapons of mass destruction, or obtaining them from other countries'.[31] On the issue of 'possible missile transfers' from North Korea, Myanmar officials responded that Yangon had 'not accepted offers of such weapons systems'.[32] Congressional testimony given by State Department officials supported Myanmar's account, including the point that there was no evidence to support claims that Myanmar was financing weapons purchases with heroin sales.[33] Considering also Myanmar's positive record on international disarmament,[34] Australian defence analyst Andrew Selth suggested that Yangon had probably acquired some defensive surface-to-air missiles from North Korea but no short-range ballistic missiles that could threaten Thailand.[35] Although the US is monitoring the situation, the investigation into these matters had not yet come up with anything new by August 2005.[36] Talks between Myanmar and Russia's atomic energy agency seemed to have resumed in October 2005, however, with a cooperation blueprint reportedly signed during Maung Aye's visit to Russia in April 2006.[37] Meanwhile, Myanmar and North Korea have apparently restored diplomatic relations.[38]

Myanmar and the second Bush term

At her Senate confirmation hearing in January 2005, Rice labelled Myanmar one of several 'outposts of tyranny'. Washington subsequently continued the rhetoric of moral castigation, while also arguing, and acting on, the point that Myanmar poses a threat to regional stability. In essence, Washington's argument is that the deterioration of the human-rights situation in Myanmar has caused general domestic conditions to deteriorate, which has ramifications for international peace and security. This argument represents a major development. During the Clinton presidency, at the time of the release of the 1998 East Asia Strategy, when problems on the border with Thailand were widely judged to be severe, the US did not make such a case.[39] This stance was rearticulated in 1999 against the backdrop of the UN-backed and US-supported International Force for East Timor intervention by then-secretary of defense William Cohen.[40] Washington seems committed to implementing methodically its revised approach.

In June 2005, Washington tried but failed to place Myanmar on the agenda of the UNSC. At the subsequent ASEAN PMC and ARF meetings, US Deputy Secretary of State Robert Zoellick referred to Myanmar as a 'cancer' that could spread to the wider region.[41] In October 2005, the US administration claimed the publication of the Havel–Tutu report and the continued denial of access for Razali and the UN Special Rapporteur for Human Rights Paulo Sérgio Pinheiro warranted the UNSC discussing the situation in Myanmar.[42] President Bush received at the Oval Office activist Charm Tong, who is associated with the Shan Women's Action Network – which claimed in 2002 that the Tatmadaw was systematically using sexual violence against ethnic-minority women along the border.[43] Beyond markedly impressing the president, she also met with National Security Advisor Stephen Hadley.[44] In November 2005, Rice criticised Asian countries for not speaking out against the Yangon regime,[45] and President Bush discussed Myanmar with leaders from Japan, Russia and China during his travels to Asia to participate in the APEC Leaders' Summit. Suggesting that the 'people of Burma live in the darkness of tyranny',[46] and its government not only represents 'Asia's past' but also 'sows instability abroad', the president also raised Myanmar with Malaysia, then-ASEAN chair, and other ASEAN leaders in an apparent bid to reinvigorate Washington's multilateral strategy towards Myanmar.

On the understanding that it had the support of eight, if not nine, states to place Myanmar on the agenda, the US successfully proposed that UNSC members organise an informal briefing, held in mid-December 2005, on what Washington saw as the 'deteriorating political, humanitarian and human rights situation' in Myanmar. US Ambassador to the UN John Bolton regarded this as only a first step. Meanwhile, Assistant Secretary of State for East Asian and Pacific Affairs Christopher Hill, outlined an alternative to the 'sham' NC and the 'empty promise' of the road map: the release of political prisoners, dialogue with the opposition, opening the NC to the full participation of all *and* UN help in facilitating a peaceful transition. Waiting for 'tangible, verifiable, and irreversible steps towards a genuine national dialogue',[47] the US is committed to advocating further UNSC scrutiny and action. The analogy invoked for a possible UNSC resolution is the situation in Iraq just after the first Gulf War. Hill and other State Department officials have thus emphasised the notion that the military regime constitutes a threat not only to Myanmar's citizens, but also to its neighbours and the broader region.[48] Myanmar is clearly not the sole target for US 'transformational diplomacy', which is about the promotion of democracy, good governance and bringing about responsible behaviour of others in the international system with the help of America's partners.[49] The second Bush administration has so far been more concerned with Iraq, Iran and North Korea than with Myanmar. However, the administration is engaged at the highest level and has increasingly made Myanmar, which it considers to be 'out of step with the entire modern experience of Southeast Asia', a priority talking point in discussions with regional governments and Myanmar's main partners.

Myanmar's diplomatic counter-offensive

Formal discussion of Myanmar by the UNSC would constitute a serious diplomatic defeat and a significant foreign-policy challenge for Yangon. The passing of a binding UNSC resolution would further amplify this challenge. Until 2005 UNSC involvement was widely regarded as rather unlikely, although US-based Burmese exiles, several international non-governmental organisations (NGOs) and various policy-makers around the globe had called for it, particularly from 2003 onwards. Accordingly, Yangon had not been much perturbed by early US indications that Washington would under no circumstances recognise any constitution emerging from the military-controlled NC.[50] But at the same time, the regime seems not to have fully discounted its long-standing fear of US intervention in view of the NATO intervention in Kosovo in 1999 and the invasion of Iraq in March 2003. In an apparent effort both to deter and discredit the US, the regime has argued that 'recent developments in Iraq and Afghanistan are ... classic examples of how wrong things could end up when the respective political histories, cultures, and security needs of a country are ... ignored in making a transition to democracy by forces from outside'.[51] The junta's official mouthpiece, the *New Light of Myanmar*, includes a regular update on the US body count in Iraq. Meanwhile, the SPDC is apparently preparing for intervention scenarios involving external agitation of its citizens, alliances of convenience between Western countries and insurgent armies and even multinational coalitions.[52] Massive bunkers have reportedly been constructed to shield the air force's MiG-29s.[53] One item on the agenda of the visit by Maung Aye to Moscow in April 2006 was the SPDC's interest in an air-defence system (in exchange for access to oil and gas resources). Some even attribute the relocation of military headquarters and ministries to Naypyidaw to a continuing fear of military intervention.[54] For the moment, the military junta is nevertheless clear that the immediate challenge is a diplomatic rather than a military one. However, the SPDC has presumably noticed that the US has emphatically pointed to UNSC Resolution 688, a resolution on the basis of which the US and UK established no-fly zones over Iraq, as a model for a possible way forward with Myanmar.

Myanmar's diplomatic counter-offensive has so far had two main elements. First, the foreign ministry has rejected in its entirety the Havel–Tutu report, arguing that had the situation in Myanmar posed a threat to regional security, its neighbours and ASEAN would surely have noticed it and called for action. To further discredit the report, the government has pointed to its similarities with a 2003 submission to the UNSC from the NCGUB.[55] The government has also sought to discredit the remaining armed ethnic groups, particularly the SSA-South, by claiming that the latter is responsible for using child soldiers and illicit narcotics deals. Second, having been encouraged by both China and Russia blocking initial moves by the US to place Myanmar on the UNSC agenda in June 2005, the military government has sought a commitment from Beijing and Moscow for extended diplomatic protection. Through its mass media, the SPDC has suggested that the US is anxious and in a rush to install a puppet government in Myanmar with the apparent intention of checking China's growing regional influence. The government held out the possibility of a major long-term gas deal with China just days before the UNSC briefing in December 2005. By also strengthening economic cooperation and leveraging its energy resources in its relations with Russia, the SPDC has sought to secure the favour of a second veto state at the UNSC. While Yangon would hope that China and Russia would block a UNSC vote on any substantive matter relating to Myanmar, its leaders appreciate that US pressure on Beijing and Moscow to abstain on any such vote is bound to increase. Neither China nor Russia sees Myanmar in isolation from other issues in their relations with the United States. This leaves Myanmar in a potentially precarious position *vis-à-vis* the United States.

Foreign policy towards Japan

From the viewpoint of Myanmar's military leaders, Japanese policy towards Yangon has been in opposition to that of the United States. Japan's approach towards Myanmar has differed from that of the United States in that Tokyo has sought to promote democratisation and human rights by essentially working for improvements through engagement and quiet dialogue with the regime. Given its less vocal and punitive position regarding Myanmar, Tokyo has thus, in theory, represented for the military an easier target than its Western counterparts from which to obtain much-needed development aid, particularly after the military leadership heeded Tokyo's 1987 call to initiate market economy reforms to prevent Japan from having to cut its ODA. Also, Myanmar and Japan had a special relationship even before the Second World War, encapsulated in Tokyo's training of the famous '30 comrades', including Aung San and Ne Win. In Yangon's view, the Japanese have retained a senti-mental attachment to Myanmar and probably some guilt for what transpired during the war. By the end of Myanmar's socialist era in 1988, Japan was its most significant donor country. From the beginning of Japan's assistance programme in the 1950s to 1988, Myanmar received more than US$2bn in grants and loans.[56] Although Tokyo suspended its development programme for Myanmar in September 1988 in reaction to the SLORC's takeover, 'old' projects were resumed in February 1989. All these factors suggested that Myanmar's chances to satisfy Tokyo's preconditions for a resumption of aid should have been reasonably good, particularly if the military decided to play its foreign-policy trump card of lifting restrictions on ASSK.

In the event, the SPDC has not succeeded in influencing Japan to change its post-1988 stance on Myanmar, especially regarding ODA. Twice, and particularly in 1995, the military leadership hoped that the release of ASSK from house arrest would be viewed as a sufficiently important development to prod Tokyo to listen to voices within Japan arguing for fuller engagement with the military regime for commercial or strategic reasons.[57] Significantly, Tokyo did welcome the 1995 release as 'substantive progress towards the realization of democracy and the improvement of the human rights situation in Myanmar'.[58] However, the possibility of fundamentally re-evaluating assistance was foreclosed because ASSK asked Tokyo to defer its decision on ODA provision. Japan merely opted to consider and implement projects that would address basic human needs. ASSK's second release in 2002 produced essentially the same outcome.

Economic relations between Myanmar and Japan have nevertheless been beneficial to the military government. Until 2003 Japan provided grant-in-aid to Myanmar for debt relief whenever Yangon managed to pay off interest and capital on ODA loans contracted up to 1988. The grant-in-aid for debt relief was intended to have the same effect as debt annulment. Though Myanmar's debt to Japan stood at approximately US$2.5bn in 2006, given the human-rights situation and the SPDC's slow pace in implementing democracy, Tokyo has felt it inappropriate to proceed with regular debt cancellation. In 2000, the SPDC informally asked Japan for US$1.45bn in assistance under the Miyazawa Plan, which offered assistance to countries affected by the Asian financial crisis. In the event, Yangon was not considered eligible, as it failed to fulfil key criteria.[59] Myanmar has nevertheless benefited from technical cooperation aid and has also received fairly broadly conceived humanitarian assistance from Japan, including assistance for safety improvements at Yangon's airport. Under the Japanese initiative for the development of the Mekong Region (from 2004 to present) Myanmar has been receiving grant aid for afforestation and improved health care services. The Japanese government also has a small-scale grant programme, the so-called Grassroots Grants Assistance; grant recipients are NGOs, research and medical institutions. While the suspension of ODA has affected Japanese business, the regime has retained Tokyo's support for trade and capital investment into major industrial projects that Myanmar is unable to finance itself.[60] Cumulative Japanese direct investment from the period from 1998–2003 stood at US$212.57m.[61] One of the largest investors is Nippon Oil Exploration (Myanmar) (NOEX), which has acquired a stake in offshore areas in which the Yetagun gas field was later discovered. With the withdrawal in September 2003 of Premier Oil, NOEX acquired further rights to Blocks M-12/13/14 off the Tanintharyi coast. Other Japanese companies invested in Myanmar include Mitsui, as a joint venture partner of the government in Mingaladon Industrial Park, which has had further interests, for instance, in steel and the Yadana gas project.

While Japan has not succumbed to US pressure to follow Washington in imposing more severe economic sanctions, this is not necessarily Yangon's achievement. Tokyo's overall policy and broadly conceived humanitarian assistance stem in part from the desire to retain as much as possible of its once pre-eminent economic role in Myanmar. Also, contrary to their US counterparts, Japanese officials have not been shy in admitting that Tokyo has geopolitical interests in Myanmar, particularly in the context of China's rising power. Within Japan, advocates of fuller engagement have not, however, won the policy debate on Myanmar outright. The 'ASSK factor' in Japanese public opinion and Japan–US relations has constrained attempts to promote a policy shift. Consequently, Yangon has found that Japan's support has remained limited. As Myanmar proceeded in the late 1990s with a spate of positive steps to address international concerns, also in response to Tokyo's prodding that the SPDC deal constructively with the ICRC and the ILO, Japan offered only diplomatic support such as suggesting the postponement of ILO measures against Myanmar.

Tokyo's reaction to ASSK's second release from house arrest seemed to indicate an interest in promoting a balanced approach towards the military and ASSK, in that the Japanese government also expected her to play a 'constructive role' in full national reconciliation, which the SPDC might have interpreted as a criticism of her previous provocations. Tokyo also announced 'emergency assistance' for renovating the Baluchanung No. 2 Hydropower Plant, which had been originally financed by Japan in 1960. In August 2002, Foreign Minister Yoriko Kawaguchi made the first visit to Myanmar by an incumbent Japanese foreign minister for 19 years. She re-emphasised Japan's historical affinity with Myanmar, again acknowledged the country's geopolitical importance and pointedly summarised Japan's position towards the regime as involving the promotion of democracy *and* nation-building. However, with reference to the need for dialogue with ASSK, Tokyo signalled only its preparedness to expand its assistance in the field of basic human needs in response to further positive moves by the SPDC towards political reconciliation.[62] Japan also agreed to Myanmar's suggestion to help fund poppy eradication in the Wa region of Shan State. Overall, however, Myanmar was again unable to decouple Tokyo's willingness to provide economic assistance from ASSK's support for such a development.

Post-Depayin relations

After June 2003, Myanmar's ties with Tokyo became more strained, arguably reflecting a growing sense of mutual estrangement. Kawaguchi had initially played down the Depayin incident, but Tokyo, responding to international and domestic public opinion, suspended new grants and technical assistance.[63] Having previously seen merit in Japan's foreign policy towards Myanmar as being 'different' from that of the US and

EU, Tokyo's more openly critical tone cast doubt on the usefulness of this distinction. Japanese Prime Minister Junichiro Koizumi emerged on the sidelines of the 2003 ASEAN Summit as the only East Asian head of government to take Khin Nyunt to task. Using the occasion of the ASEAN–Japan Commemorative Summit in December 2003, Khin Nyunt reminded Tokyo that from Yangon's perspective Japanese assistance was insufficient. The following January, Japan lifted part of its 2003 freeze on assistance, not least when it offered the SPDC scholarships for human-resources development,[64] with a larger amount being made available for the same purpose in June. The larger conflict over ASSK continued nonetheless, and Myanmar's regime was also dissatisfied with Japan's inadequate support for the NC, though this dissatisfaction was rarely articulated in public. However, the SPDC denied Japan its public backing in Tokyo's diplomatic campaign for permanent membership of the UNSC, either as part of the Group of Four (Japan, India, Germany and Brazil) or individually. The rationale for this decision was that such public support of Tokyo's position would have antagonised Beijing. It stood in contrast to the SPDC's explicit backing for India's UNSC membership, indicating the significance of New Delhi and the present peripheral importance of Tokyo in the regime's foreign policy.

Myanmar's decision-makers may have believed that to advance relations with Japan they could build on a shared history and exploit the competitive dynamics of the regional balance of power, which they see as compelling all major Asian powers to pursue a strategy of active engagement with Yangon. However, the regime has found Tokyo much more critical of its domestic politics than China and India, particularly regarding ASSK. Significantly, though, the Koizumi government had not by April 2006 backed US diplomatic rhetoric that Myanmar's freedom needs to be advanced because the regime's policies and practices constitute a threat to international and regional peace and security. In December 2005, as UNSC members were briefed on the situation in Myanmar by Gambari, Japan agreed with China and Russia that they did not.

European Union

It is not evident that Myanmar has designed a well-considered strategy towards Europe. It has certainly not demonstrated interest either in pursuing sustained, active diplomatic lobbying to persuade European governments to reconsider their Common Position or to prevent the imposition of new sanctions. Myanmar has similarly not seriously attempted to exploit small but noticeable differences in the respective national positions between, say, the British and Danes, and the Germans and French. Nor has the regime employed professional lobbyists to influence European policy decisions on Myanmar, though it has used them in the US. Moreover, Yangon has not asked the European Union or the governments of its member states to mediate between the US and Myanmar. While all this could be regarded as evidence of the limited significance Europe enjoys in Myanmar's overall foreign policy, Yangon's lack of activist diplomacy towards European institutions and governments more likely reflects its appreciation of the difficulties inherent in influencing EU policy. The SPDC has to live with the fact that since the late 1980s there has been an express commitment by European governments to promote and protect human rights and fundamental freedoms, first in European Political Cooperation and, subsequently, in implementing the EU's Common Foreign and Security Policy.[65] Since 1996 and the passing of the EU Common Position on Burma/Myanmar, the military regime has been forced to deal with Europe's governments as a grouping. How Myanmar could produce a shift in the consensual position of 25 members is indeed difficult to see. One consequence of Europe having a Common Position has incidentally also been that countries regarded during the Ne Win period as good friends (such as Germany) have lost significance and standing in Yangon.

Three objectives may be said to have driven Myanmar's foreign policy towards Europe since the late 1990s. One has been to seek to improve Myanmar's image. While appreciating that Myanmar would be unable to change European public opinion, Khin Nyunt and his advisers hoped that targeted information campaigns would induce law-makers and perhaps even European decision-makers to adopt a more understanding and productive position on Myanmar. A second related objective has focused not on a full resumption of development aid, but on winning more humanitarian assistance and receiving human resources training. Yangon has also hoped to dissuade the Europeans from tightening the sanctions regime by imposing, like the Americans, a ban on new investments or a trade embargo. (In 2005 EU exports to Myanmar totalled €83m [€77m in 2004], while imports from Myanmar totalled €287m [€460m in 2004]).[66] The political sanctions imposed on the regime by the EU are not of great concern in Myanmar. Though the SPDC probably finds the visa ban irritating, it would seem that its main impact has been to generate disappointment.[67] The third objective regarding Europe has focused on winning admission – despite strong European objections – to the two major inter-regional dialogues that the EU has with ASEAN and the wider Asia (ASEAN–EU and ASEM).

Limited achievements

Myanmar has failed to make substantial headway in improving relations with Europe, although a critical dialogue between the two sides was again in the making by early 2005. Notably, while the news of secret discussions between the regime and ASSK initially proved beneficial and helped to ensure U Win Aung's first-ever participation at the ASEAN–EU Ministerial Meeting in December 2000, the period of political relaxation and domestic confidence-building under Khin Nyunt did not bring more than limited political or economic benefit, as the EU was reluctant to revise its overall assessment of the situation in Myanmar. Based on the report of a director-general-level EU Troika to Myanmar in late January 2001, for instance, the EU found no 'substantive progress towards the objectives set out in the Common Position'.[68] As the political climate in Myanmar improved further, the Council of the European Union amended its Common Position so that visas could be issued to Myanmar state representatives on UN business or by dint of a waiver to be agreed by all members 'where it is in the interests of the European Union'.[69] The 2002 release of ASSK was welcomed, but the Council expressed disappointment soon afterwards about the failure to start a wider political process,[70] essentially a dialogue between government, the NLD and ethnic minorities. The lack of substantive political gain derived from ASSK's second release was underscored in April 2003 when the Council threatened to implement by 29 October 2003 a new set of measures in the absence of the following: the commencement of a 'substantive dialogue' between the authorities, ASSK and the democratic movement; the release of political prisoners; the 'complete freedom of action and movement' for ASSK; and a reduction of the violence and human-rights violations in Myanmar, particularly in ethnic-minority areas.[71] With the Europeans having stressed that they would 'continue to react proportionately to developments in Burma/Myanmar, either positive or negative',[72] Yangon was unable to avoid a tightening of EU political sanctions in the aftermath of Depayin. Given the political capital invested by the regime, and particularly by the Secretary-1, in reaching accommodation with ASSK and in improving ties with EU member states, the SPDC considered the Council's response limited and politically damaging to Khin Nyunt. As with the US and Japan, the EU's answer to the SPDC's political gamble was that unless the regime treated ASSK as an equal and acceded to a substantial dialogue on the terms she and the West demanded, major improvements in bilateral relations were unlikely.[73] In line with its political-security imperative, Myanmar has not given in to EU demands, before or since Depayin.

Having demonstrably failed to enhance their regime's image, Yangon's diplomats have had some success in securing EU assistance to address the country's serious humanitarian situation. The European Commission Humanitarian Aid Office (ECHO) has since 1994 regularly made available funds for vulnerable people, not only along the Thai–Myanmar border but also within Myanmar itself. From 2001 to 2004 ECHO tripled its annual funding to €19.4m. In 2005, the EU declared that it would expand financial assistance to €30–35m to assist Myanmar in relevant areas.[74] The EU Common Position of 25 October 2004 specifically allows for projects and programmes on health and education as well as poverty alleviation and the environment. In 2005, ECHO committed €16.5m,[75] and also agreed to set up an office in Yangon. Individual member states have also pursued humanitarian goals in Myanmar. The UK's Department for International Development, for instance, has funded several projects in Myanmar to help particular Millennium Development Goals (relating to poverty, hunger, primary schooling, child mortality, gender and diseases).[76]

There has been no impetus within the EU to follow the US example by imposing a trade freeze. In 2004, the EU was Myanmar's fourth largest trade partner. Existing European investments remain unaffected by the EU Common Position, although some European governments have exerted moral pressure on companies to withdraw from Myanmar. The French company Total is the largest European investor; it has been involved in the Yadana gas project, the controversial construction of a pipeline to Thailand, and in 2005 was one of six foreign companies to have signed offshore joint production contracts with the MOGE.[77]

Notwithstanding its problems in its relations with Europe, in 2004 Myanmar finally joined ASEM at its summit in Hanoi in 2004, albeit not at the level of heads of state/government. Though this was a significant achievement insofar as it occurred despite the Depayin incident and Yangon's decision to abandon the second meeting of the Bangkok Process in April 2004, as well as its refusal to release ASSK and U Tin Oo, Myanmar's participation at the Hanoi Summit was not primarily the SPDC's achievement. That honour belongs to Vietnam, the chair. Still, from a diplomatic perspective, Myanmar played its cards well when it agreed to Hanoi's proposal to accept lower-level representation. Myanmar could then rely on Hanoi to prevail over objections from some quarters to make this, first, the consensual ASEAN position and, subsequently, the joint ASEAN+3 position. Eventually, the European side also acquiesced given that not only the Hanoi summit, but also the ASEM process was threatened given disagreements over Myanmar's participation.[78] For Myanmar, this was a positive development both in the sense that it enhanced its international legitimacy, whatever the European protestations to the contrary, while simultaneously forcing the Europeans to move beyond a policy of isolating and excluding it.

Europe as a continuing foreign policy challenge

Yangon's foreign policy still aims for improvement in Myanmar–EU relations. Officials in the Ministry of Foreign Affairs know that the EU position on Myanmar is far from uncontroversial among European governments and institutions (Council, Commission, Parliament), given both the political stalemate in Myanmar and the humanitarian situation.[79] At the 15th ASEAN–EU Ministerial Meeting in March 2005, the EU re-embarked on what External Relations Commissioner Benita Ferrero-Waldner referred to as 'constructive but at the same time critical' direct dialogue. A bilateral meeting between the EU Troika and Nyan Win in Jakarta, as envisaged by Ferrero-Waldner, did not come to pass, however, as Nyan Win did not attend.[80] This was followed by a 'Burma Day' conference organised in Brussels in early April, which discussed a report written for the Commission that argued for new ways forward to meet the needs of Myanmar's population.[81] In other words, European countries have opted to concentrate more than before on ameliorating the humanitarian situation in Myanmar while pursuing critical engagement.

As part of this critical engagement, Europe has continued to challenge Myanmar, not least in the context of inter-regional relations. At the 7th ASEM Foreign Ministers' Meeting in Kyoto in May 2005, U Nyan Win reportedly accepted the Japanese invitation to respond to criticisms from the Europeans by taking the floor during the formal exchanges to appraise his colleagues of unfolding developments in Myanmar. On the sidelines of the ASEM meeting, Ferrero-Waldner and Luxembourg Foreign Minister Jean Asselborn handed Nyan Win a list of political detainees that they asked to be released immediately, including ASSK, for reasons of justice and humanitarian considerations. Myanmar responded by opening a consulate in Brussels, to allow for better representation of its policies. With the opening of an embassy in Belgium, Myanmar is also appointing a representative to the EU.

Interestingly, Myanmar's diplomats are nevertheless pessimistic about achieving fundamentally better relations with Europe. From the regime's viewpoint, the UK remains the chief obstacle to better relations, due to the standing ASSK enjoys in London owing to her personal connections with British officials and the fact that her sons are British citizens. The regime

also believes that the concerns and sentiments expressed by UK parliamentarians over the suffering of ethnic groups, particularly the Karen/Kayin,
are linked not only to colonial history, but also to a British sense of guilt and
Christian solidarity. Suspicions run deep that the British continue to seek
to deny Myanmar its rightful place in international society and a political
solution to its problems. It came as no surprise when the UK joined the US
in asking that the issue of Myanmar be placed on the UNSC agenda.

Conclusion

Myanmar's foreign policy towards the US, Japan and Europe has tended to
be more reactive than proactive and more defiant than cooperative on what
the West and Japan have regarded as their key political demands. Yangon's
perspective is that the West's willingness to reward Myanmar for moving
towards political reconciliation has proved far less pronounced than its
propensity to punish. Given the perceived domestic political-security
imperative, this has reinforced views that repeating the political and
foreign policy experiment undertaken by Khin Nyunt between 2000 and
2003 would not be worthwhile. However, the SPDC's determination instead
to implement the road map without the participation of ASSK and the NLD
is in turn politically unpalatable to the US, the EU and Japan. Moreover,
Yangon's open defiance and intransigence have not been helpful in the face
of Bush's argument that the 'demands of justice, and the peace of this world'
require Myanmar's freedom.[82] Though differences in their respective policies towards Myanmar continue to characterise the positions of the West
and Japan, this does not really matter in the UNSC context. The UK and
France, together with European non-permanent members of the UNSC, are
likely to support another call for Myanmar to be placed on the agenda and
are unlikely to object to the kind of demands Washington would like to see
enveloped in an initial UNSC mandate. Japan's stance on this issue appears
more uncertain, given its attempt to secure permanent membership of the
UNSC and its attendant desire to accommodate contrasting concerns, but
Tokyo does not have a good track record of resisting US pressure and will
have to take its leave from the UNSC as a non-permanent member at the
end of 2006. As any UNSC resolution might envisage the UNSG playing
an important role in obliging and facilitating national reconciliation, the
question remains as to what lessons have already been learned about cooperation between Myanmar and the UN and, in particular, what Myanmar's
record of dealing with various UN organs suggests about the possibilities
for overcoming the domestic political impasse.

CHAPTER FIVE

Myanmar and the United Nations

Myanmar joined the United Nations less than four months after winning independence in January 1948, primarily to protect itself against future possible aggression by a stronger power.[1] By the end of the socialist era in 1988, Myanmar's legacy to the UN had essentially taken two forms: the executive stewardship of the UN by Secretary-General U Thant from 1961 to 1971;[2] and its unswerving commitment to neutrality and interest in working for global disarmament. After 1988, maintaining relations with UN organs and specialised agencies developed into a significant foreign-policy challenge. Myanmar has endured considerable criticism in the UNGA, the UNCHR and also in the UN-associated ILO, which had a corresponding detrimental effect on its international reputation.[3] Yet, while dissociating itself from what it considers unjust criticism, the Myanmar government has to some extent, although not consistently and not necessarily in substantive terms, adhered to its declared policy of cooperating with the United Nations in every field, including human rights.[4] Following two years of significant effort by the regime, and by Khin Nyunt in particular, the level of cooperation with the UN has significantly declined since 2003 and especially after the ouster of Khin Nyunt in 2004. At the core of Myanmar's relations with the UN have stood the good offices role of the UNSG and cooperation with the UNCHR, especially its special rapporteur. The involvement of the UNSC from December 2005 opened a new chapter in Myanmar's foreign policy, but with no clear outcome in prospect.

Dealing with the UNGA and the UNCHR

In 1991, for the first time the UNGA passed a resolution on the situation in Myanmar; since 1993 the focus has been on human rights in the country. The UNCHR has focused on Myanmar since 1992, establishing the post of special rapporteur. The annual UNGA resolutions initially called on the SLORC to take all necessary steps to restore democracy in line with the election results of 1990 and to allow all citizens to participate in the political process in accordance with the Universal Declaration of Human Rights. The 1992 UNGA resolution contained the UN's first explicit call for Yangon to release ASSK. The following year, the UNGA filed its first critical assessment of the NC. The list of recommendations and demands made by the UNGA and the UNCHR has grown considerably over the years. After ASSK's 1995 release from house arrest, the UNGA repeatedly urged the SLORC regime to free other detained political leaders and to engage in a substantive political dialogue aimed at democratisation and national reconciliation with the NLD, its general secretary and other opposition figures, including leaders of the ethnic-minority groups. In addition, the Myanmar authorities have increasingly stood accused of a growing list of human-rights violations including extra-judicial killings, rape and other forms of sexual violence carried out by members of the armed forces; torture; renewed instances of political arrests and continuing detentions; forced relocation; destruction of livelihoods; forced labour; denial of freedoms of assembly, association, expression and movement; discrimination on the basis of religious or ethnic background; wide disrespect for the rule of law and lack of independence for the judiciary; deeply unsatisfactory conditions of detention; systematic use of child soldiers; and even violations of rights to adequate living standards. During 2004–05 UNGA resolutions have expressed grave concern at the 'ongoing systematic violation' of human rights; the events of 30 May 2003 and the continuing detention and house arrest of ASSK; Myanmar's failure to implement recommendations contained in past UNGA and UNCHR resolutions; and restrictions placed on the NLD. Demands made on Myanmar include an end to human-rights violations; an inclusive NC; an inquiry into the events at Depayin; an end to the recruitment and use of child soldiers and 'systematic enforced displacement of persons'; as well as a clear and detailed plan for a transition to democracy, including its timing.[5]

Myanmar's basic response to such condemnations of its human-rights record and attendant recommendations has been informed by its interpretation of the sanctity of Article 2, Paragraph 7 of the UN Charter; in other words, the SPDC has considered them to constitute an infringement of the principle of non-interference. In particular, it has considered its national reconciliation process to be an internal affair. Its principled position notwithstanding, it has been the foreign policy of the government not to leave allegations of human-rights violations wholly unanswered. Hence, since first being subjected to international criticism in the UNCHR and the Third Committee of the UNGA, Myanmar's delegation leaders have consistently rejected a significant number of alleged human-rights violations and dissociated themselves from resolutions. They have made no bones about finding draft proposals on the situation of human rights in Myanmar to be one sided, as well as characterised by subjective judgements and politically motivated allegations. In Myanmar's view, many allegations of human-rights violations also remain unsubstantiated and 'grossly exaggerated'.[6] Its officials have particularly vehemently denied the use of rape as a weapon, as well as the use of child soldiers.

Interestingly, at no point until 2005 did Yangon attempt to press for a vote on any draft resolution, with the consequence that the UNGA and the UNCHR, since 1991 and 1992 respectively, have adopted resolutions on the human rights situation in Myanmar by consensus. Myanmar's diplomats seemingly opted for this path because they considered it best not to squander valuable diplomatic support by asking for public backing. They instead concentrated on opportunities to amend draft formulations perceived as grossly insulting or as raising concerns about national or regime security. Ultimately, this method allowed Myanmar to escape neither the increasingly incriminating language, including accusations of 'systematic' violations, nor the growing list of demands to redress the human-rights situation. However, Myanmar's approach has enjoyed some success. For instance, whereas UNGA resolutions from 1991 successively called for the recognition and 'early implementation' of the 1990 election results, the 2004 resolution merely called on the regime to 'respect the results' of that election by, inter alia, releasing the NLD leadership.[7] Also, by 2004, there were no Asian co-sponsors of the UNGA resolution, in contrast to earlier years.[8] Nevertheless, Myanmar has routinely criticised the unbalanced nature of the annual draft resolution, at times highlighting omissions regarding measures taken to improve the human-rights situation or accusing the co-sponsors of relying on information collected by anti-regime forces.

In 2005, however, in the context of looming UNSC involvement, Myanmar became concerned over the potential political damage inflicted by yet another UNGA resolution. Consequently, in 2005 Myanmar relied on Cuba to table a motion requesting the adjournment of the debate in the

UN Third Committee to prevent the passing of a further UNGA resolution. The motion was defeated by 77 to 54, with 35 abstentions.[9] In the end, the draft resolution was again adopted by consensus.

A major aspect of Myanmar's cooperation with the UN on human rights has included working with the UNHRC special rapporteur, even though Myanmar formally dissociated itself from the decision to establish this mandate. According to Resolution 1992/58 of 3 March 1992 the terms of reference for the special rapporteur are: 'to establish direct contacts with the Government and with the people of Myanmar, including political leaders deprived of their liberty, their families and lawyers, with a view to examining the situation of human rights in Myanmar and following any progress made towards the transfer of power to a civilian government and drafting of a new constitution, the lifting of restrictions on personal freedoms and the restoration of human rights in Myanmar'.[10] Special rapporteurs have included Japanese Professor Yozo Yokota (1992–96), Mauritius Chief Justice Rajsoomer Lallah (1996–2000) and Brazilian Professor Paulo Sérgio Pinheiro (since December 2000). As early as 1990, the SLORC accepted a visit by Sagato Ogata in her capacity as an independent expert sent by the UNCHR. Cooperation extended to the special rapporteurs has varied considerably, depending largely on whether the SPDC-led government has perceived their respective reports to be fair and balanced.

Myanmar's leaders cooperated in various ways with Yokata, allowing him to visit Myanmar on several occasions, but they regularly denied him the opportunity to meet ASSK until after restrictions were lifted on her in July 1995. When they did allow for his visit in October 1995, they appeared troubled by his critical assessment of the human-rights situation, insofar as the special rapporteur repeated and expanded on previous recommendations and also concluded that the NC, which was to be reconvened in November 1995, did not appear to constitute the necessary 'steps towards the restoration of democracy, fully respecting the will of the people as expressed in the democratic elections held in 1990', as stated in UNGA Resolution 47/144, Paragraph 4. If the SPDC's verdict on Yokota was ultimately unfavourable, its working relationship with his successor, Lallah, was insubstantial. Yangon accused Lallah of political bias and repeatedly denied his request even to visit Myanmar. His 1997 report was rejected on the grounds that it 'only reproduced the litany of complaints that invariably emanated from dubious and politically motivated sources', adding that 'unrestrained criticisms and diatribes against the Myanmar Government are unjustified, untimely and counterproductive'.[11] Significantly, Lallah also directly questioned the political role of the armed forces in the proposed new constitutional system.[12] He dismissed Yangon's complaints over intrusiveness and interference, and accused the regime of an 'attitude of non-cooperation'. His unflattering assessment led to the further strengthening of resolutions against Myanmar, a development then also exploited by Albright, who painted a picture of Myanmar as an international pariah. Myanmar dismissed this as misleading given that all draft resolutions has been adopted without a vote. Yangon's permanent representative, U Win Mra, also strongly rejected Albright's contention that Myanmar had refused to cooperate with the UN.[13] That said, until the end of his tenure, the SPDC saw no benefit from a visit by the special rapporteur.

By contrast, in the context of the wind of change unleashed by Khin Nyunt, Pinheiro was allowed to visit Myanmar for six fact-finding missions, starting in April 2001. The SPDC initially provided what it and Pinheiro himself considered to be 'full and unhindered cooperation' during his visits to Myanmar.[14] This involved meetings with the military leadership and the NLD, as well as visits to various locations inside the country. The Myanmar government initially also voiced its satisfaction at Pinheiro's more nuanced assessments of the country's human-rights situation; indeed, his 2002 report was described as 'fairly balanced', although some aspects, such as religious persecution against non-Buddhists, were rejected.[15] The regime appreciated, moreover, Pinheiro's call for the international community to support efforts towards Myanmar's 'principled engagement'. Symbolic of its willingness to cooperate with the UN, Pinheiro's visits to Myanmar usually produced concrete gestures, often involving the release of political and other prisoners. Shortly after his fourth visit in October 2002, for example, the government freed from detention several hundred women on humanitarian grounds. One issue that the regime prevented the special rapporteur from investigating was the allegation of the military's systematic rape of Shan women, which the leadership strongly denied. As the reconciliation process with ASSK faltered, the military articulated its disappointment that the cooperation extended to Pinheiro had failed to translate into an even more balanced 'tone and thrust' despite the 'significant developments in Myanmar [in 2002/03]' which were considered 'more substantive and numerous than at any time before'.[16] In March 2003, Pinheiro discovered a microphone during a routine interview with a political prisoner in Insein jail, causing him to break off his visit. Some observers suggest that having lost face over the bugging incident and Pinheiro's demand for an apology, Yangon subsequently found dealing with him more difficult.

The events of Depayin did not immediately end cooperation between the SPDC and Pinheiro, even though he filed a report in August 2003 arguing that the 'May 30-related developments have constituted a potentially terminal setback on the political front and, for that matter, for the human rights situation in the country'.[17] Responding to his request to conduct an independent assessment of the Depayin incident, and perhaps thinking it was best for him to inform himself of the situation after the announcement of the road map, Yangon again invited Pinheiro to Myanmar in November 2003. With the regime's full cooperation, he visited ASSK and three other NLD leaders still placed under house arrest, as part of his investigation into the events of 30 May. Whether the SPDC expected Pinheiro to reach conclusions favourable to the regime is unclear; it did not happen, however. He concluded that 'there is prima facie evidence that the Depayin incident could not have happened without the connivance of State agents'.[18] In the same report, Pinheiro argued that human-rights principles should guide the road map during the *whole* process of its implementation and, therefore, called for the lifting of all remaining restrictions on expression, movement, information, assembly and association, the removal of related 'security' legislation, and the re-opening of all political parties' offices throughout the country. He moreover called for the immediate restoration of the freedom of movement and political activity of ASSK and other political leaders of the NLD to secure their early participation in the first stage of the NC. Significantly, Pinheiro even suggested that delegates to the NC should 'represent the full range of political parties and ethnic- minority groups and should proportionally reflect the results of the 1990 elections'.[19] These recommendations were not exactly music to the ears of the SPDC, nor were some of Pinheiro's other remarks, notwithstanding his evident attempts to remain balanced and fair in his formal assessments. In June 2004, for instance, he was quoted in the press as saying that the situation of NC participants amounted to 'house arrest'.[20] He later nevertheless described the NC as a 'potentially significant step towards national reconciliation and political transition' given that it has secured the participation of a large number of ethnic nationalities, including ceasefire groups.[21] In his August 2005 interim report, Pinheiro argued that the transition to a full, participatory and democratic system in Myanmar could no longer be postponed. He also warned that failure to redress the NC's procedural limitations would render the emerging constitution void of legitimacy and credibility.[22] His 2006 report to the UNCHR argued that any progress towards resolving ethnic conflict in Myanmar is unlikely to be possible or sustainable without tangible political reform.[23] The military leadership clearly disagrees with this analysis and the criticisms by the special rapporteur regarding the NC and its modalities and, since 2003, the lack of dialogue with ASSK, the NLD and the ethnic-minority groups. Neither are they negotiable given the military's perceived political-security imperative. Citing its inability to find mutually convenient dates, the government has thus since November 2003 not invited Pinheiro to conduct another fact-finding mission in Myanmar. This has left the special rapporteur dissatisfied, and led to his conclusion that the 'positive momentum' evident in the early years of his appointment had dissipated and that the present administration is 'far less inclined towards democratic change'.[24] He has been equally blunt in his assessment that the regime had not only generally not implemented his recommendations, but also upturned many of the positive political developments seen under Khin Nyunt's tenure, illustrated by the apparent disbandment of the Human Rights Committee. It would seem that the lack of progress on human rights achieved by Myanmar has contributed elsewhere to openly articulated disdain of the powers of the UNCHR, and calls favouring the creation of a Human Rights Council with teeth, a proposal Myanmar opposed.[25] Significantly, Pinheiro did not commit himself to the statistics on human-rights abuses as contained in the Havel–Tutu report, but he has noted that the positive trends towards addressing humanitarian exigencies had been 'largely reversed' since October 2004, leaving some citizens with 'acute humanitarian needs'. With his six-year mandate coming to an end, Pinheiro is stepping down in 2006.

Cooperation with the UNSG and special envoys

Responding to a request expressed in UNGA Resolution 48/150 of 20 December 1993, UNSG Boutros Boutros-Ghali proposed in February 1994 to then-Secretary-1 Khin Nyunt the establishment of a dialogue with the UN. The SPDC accepted this proposal by the following August. The parameters of dialogue agreed in October 1994 related to: plans to return to democracy; the NC; the situation of ASSK and other political leaders; human rights and humanitarian issues; and the prospects for reintegration of 'national races' into political life.[26] Until 1999, substantive discussions on these issues involved above all Foreign Minister U Ohn Gyaw and Alvaro de Soto, formerly UN assistant secretary-general for political affairs, who visited Myanmar repeatedly. Regular meetings also took place in New York, involving the UNSG. Seeing their role essentially as one of providing good offices to further national reconciliation, the UNSG and his representative were pleased to see the lifting of restraints on ASSK in July 1995. Discussions thereafter focused on: Myanmar's embrace of a multi-party democratic system; the mandate, composition, procedures and functioning of the NC; and the role of those elected in 1990.[27] Both the UNSG and the special envoy sought to overcome the lack of progress made towards establishing a substantive dialogue between the regime, the NLD and representatives of ethnic-minority groups. The SPDC and its foreign minister consistently rejected the idea of a separate dialogue between the government and ASSK, pointing out that: the regime's priorities focused on 'national reconsolidation' and the eradication of national insurgencies; the NC was the designated dialogue forum, and that ASSK, having withdrawn the NLD delegates in late 1995, could make her views known through other delegates; and the leadership was not prepared to deal with ASSK outside the NC in a separate dialogue on an equal footing. Given the UNSG's proclaimed role of facilitating reconciliation, the SPDC found incongruity between Boutros-Ghali's disappointment over the lack of substantive dialogue on the one hand, and his apparent indifference to ASSK's strategy of confrontation on the other. The dialogue nevertheless continued with Kofi Annan, the incoming UNSG, at the highest level.

Than Shwe met Kofi Annan in Kuala Lumpur in December 1997. When de Soto next visited Myanmar in January 1998, he also had a rare meeting with the senior general. Asked by de Soto why the government felt it could adopt an inclusive approach towards the ethnic-minority armed groups but not the unarmed NLD, the government complained about ASSK's attitude, claiming it lacked sincerity and respect and was not premised on working constructively with the military. When de Soto visited Myanmar for the last time in October 1999, the SPDC bluntly rejected his idea that assistance from IFIs could be made available in return for political concessions. Told that the Myanmar leadership were not 'monkeys' that would dance when offered a banana, de Soto found his position irreparably damaged by this proposal. For five years the SPDC had regular and in-depth personal exchanges with the UNSG and his officials, but ultimately had not complied with many demands expressed in non-binding UNGA resolutions.

Razali replaced de Soto as UNSG special envoy in April 2000. Within three months of his appointment the SPDC received him in an attempt to 'build confidence'. By December 2005, he had visited Myanmar 14 times to promote national reconciliation, the last visit taking place in spring 2004. Razali's main interlocutors within the military government were then Khin Nyunt and U Win Aung. He was also always able to meet ASSK. Notably, Razali's second visit to Myanmar was in September 2000, after the military leadership and ASSK had a major disagreement, prompted by her renewed attempts to travel beyond Yangon. Having seen

UNSG Kofi Annan personally intervene on her behalf and the military quickly lift the initially imposed confinement, there was soon a second stand-off, leading to a renewed period of house arrest. Within days of Razali's second visit, and unknown to him at the time, the regime and ASSK nevertheless began secret talks. He subsequently facilitated the process of communication between her and the regime that ultimately resulted in her renewed release in May 2002. During this period, Khin Nyunt committed the government to significant cooperation with the UNSG. After Razali's third visit in January 2001, for instance, the regime released U Tin Oo and dozens of party members. At that stage the SPDC also authorised a visit by a new special rapporteur of the UNCHR.[28] Khin Nyunt also agreed to the release of political prisoners on a case-by-case basis, and followed Ambassador Razali's suggestion to allow the NLD to resume its political activities and to re-open NLD township offices. The military did not however agree with his suggestion to establish a trilateral dialogue including the ethnic minorities.[29]

In early 2002, the UN asked Myanmar to consider moving beyond confidence-building to a dialogue on substantive political issues. Myanmar, so Razali suggested, could receive considerably more humanitarian assistance from UN bodies and other parties if it did so. The SPDC complied by lifting restrictions on ASSK's freedom of movement, notwithstanding intra-SPDC disagreements over the pace of the unfolding political process. Again, though, no substantive political dialogue ensued between the SPDC and ASSK, suggesting that confidence-building between the two sides was incomplete. By March 2003 the UNSG consequently felt obliged to conclude that the reconciliation process had stalled.[30] From the government's perspective, ASSK had started to behave as if already involved in an electoral campaign, contrary to apparent tacit understandings. Her touring of the country, which the military saw as highly provocative and destabilising, engendered a backlash within the regime that ultimately resulted in the Depayin incident and ASSK's 'protective detention'.

Razali was allowed to visit ASSK after Depayin, not least to disprove international speculation about her medical condition. Khin Nyunt received Razali again only days prior to the important 2003 ASEAN Summit in Jakarta, arranging meetings with both SPDC leaders *and* ASSK once more. However, Razali failed to persuade the regime to free ASSK and he obtained no guarantee that she would be part of the road map announced by Khin Nyunt the previous August.[31] Razali learned that the NLD would need to ask to rejoin the NC, although it was hinted that the request would not be rejected.[32] His last visit to Yangon in his capacity as special envoy took place in March 2004 in advance of the NC. Occasional meetings with Razali continued, albeit only outside Myanmar, until he decided in January 2006 not to extend his contract.[33] Throwing in the towel was the logical outcome of the SPDC's unwillingness to deal further with him.

From Yangon's perspective, Razali had for some time not been facilitating the process of domestic political reconciliation. Consternation prevailed over his failure to ensure that ASSK would keep her side of the tacit political bargain struck in 2002. When, after Depayin, he gave assurances that ASSK was prepared 'to turn a new leaf', the core leadership was unmoved. Exception had, moreover, been taken to the idea that the special envoy was indispensable to Myanmar's political development. From the regime's perspective, its steps in relation to ASSK and the NLD after October 2000 had not been taken *because* of Razali, but rather because the SPDC wanted to work with the United Nations from a position of relative strength for the good of Myanmar's future. He was considered to have failed to remain impartial; the regime saw little difference between his position and those of the United States and the UK.[34] His efforts to induce China to exert influence on Myanmar, which were directly exposed by the Chinese to the highest level of Myanmar's leadership, badly damaged him in the eyes of the regime. Moreover, his public articulations of frustration did not impress either. For his part, Razali admitted to having made mistakes, such as not putting more effort into securing tangible rewards for the regime in return for the temporary liberalisation of the political climate in 2000–03.[35]

Both the UNSG and the Myanmar government find themselves in an increasingly difficult position. Especially since Depayin, Kofi Annan has had to deal with significant pressure from Burmese exiles and influential US senators to use his authority under Article 99 of the UN Charter to bring the situation in Myanmar to the attention of the UNSC.[36] In response to the SPDC's road map, which he regarded as having potential as a step towards national reconciliation, he called for Myanmar to democratise by 2006, the year in which the country was supposed to take over the ASEAN chairmanship. Although he initially welcomed the NC, he has made no bones about finding it to have fallen far short of expectations and has argued that the continued detention of ASSK and other NLD members, the detention and arrest of ethnic-minority leaders, the continued imposition of restrictions on the activities of the country's political parties, and the continued presence of large numbers of people in prison for expressing their political views are wholly incompatible with a process of democratisation and national reconciliation, 'however defined'.[37] By April 2006, the UNSG considered the refusal to allow his special envoy to visit Myanmar as casting serious doubt on the prospect of the United Nations facilitating UNGA resolutions effectively.

Despite the evident incompatibility between the SPDC's political-security imperative and the UNGA demands, the military regime has been keen not to see the UNSG concluding publicly that his good offices role has irreparably failed, as this would play into the hands of those interested in imposing a solution. It has been suggested that a visit to Myanmar by the UNSG himself might break the political ice. In April 2005, Than Shwe indeed invited Annan to visit Myanmar albeit only to allow the UNSG to see for himself the government's progress towards implementing its seven-step road map. However, Myanmar's senior officials appreciate the potential for such a visit to backfire. Naturally anything other than a 'win–win' outcome is unacceptable to them. It would appear, however, that the regime itself does not believe this can be achieved in present circumstances, and the UNSG seems to agree without admitting as much. When delivering his report on Myanmar in October 2005, Annan noted the considerable difficulties encountered in performing his good offices role since the ousting of Khin Nyunt, but remained committed to continuing his efforts. He has also stuck by his position that the seven-point road map towards democracy has the potential to generate positive change and reaffirmed the potential role of the NC as the first stage of that road map. However, urging the SPDC to take the necessary steps to make political reform efforts more inclusive and cred- ible during all phases of the road map, the UNSG effectively asked the junta by 2006 to have initiated an improved dialogue process with politi- cal leaders and representatives of ethnic minorities, released political prisoners, lifted remaining restrictions on all political leaders, reopened NLD offices and included all groups in the road map process.[38] In return, he promised to mobilise international assistance. The decision by Razali to step aside in January 2006 highlighted the extent of the challenge the UN is facing in seeking to play a good offices role. Razali has expressed scepticism whether the core leadership might invite in a new envoy.[39] A further question is, of course, whether any new envoy could achieve anything significant under the existing good offices mandate.

Myanmar, the UNSC and the possible role of the UNSG

Significantly, those who have so far argued that Myanmar poses a threat to international peace and security continue to see a role for the UNSG.[40]

For example, the Havel–Tutu report's recommendation is for the UNSC to adopt a resolution in accordance with its authority under Chapter VII (Article 41) that would, inter alia, 'require' the Myanmar government to work with the UNSG's office in implementing national reconciliation and the restoration of a democratically elected government, and allow the immediate and unconditional release of ASSK and all prisoners of conscience.[41] However, Resolution 688, which Hill identified as a possible model resolution, as it condemned the repression of the Iraqi civilian population and highlighted internal displacement and the crossborder flow of refugees as posing a regional threat, only requested the UNSG to deal with the humanitarian situation. Even assuming that the United States will be able to again muster the necessary number of potential votes, the passing of any UNSC resolution in the case of Myanmar is not a foregone conclusion. What role the UNSG's office might play in future is also unclear, but there could well be a call for the involvement of the UNSG in moving the reconciliation process forward if China and Russia were ultimately to find the text of any draft resolution amenable. This would herald a new chapter in relations between the UNSG and Myanmar.

The UNSG has never himself argued that Myanmar constitutes a threat to international peace and security, although during the informal consultations on 16 December, he qualified this by saying that while 'the situation in Myanmar did not pose an *immediate* threat to international peace and security, many issues do have crossborder implications, give cause for significant concern and could pose a threat to human security'.[42] He also expressed concern about the more restricted operational environment for UN organisations and programmes in Myanmar since October 2004 and the withdrawal of funding pledges by the Global Fund, not least because of the implications for aggravating the humanitarian situation.[43] Consequently, the UNSG has voiced disquiet over the restrictions associated with new operational guidelines for the assistance community, which were passed by the SPDC in February 2006. He has also suggested that China, India and ASEAN should take a 'leading role' in providing counsel to and accelerating reform – including political reform – in Myanmar. Not having seen his expectations regarding the potential of the road map and the NC fulfilled, the UNSG himself has proposed that the UNSC should request the consent of the Myanmar authorities to allow him to fully implement his good offices mandate, in addition to which members of the international community would coordinate an effective and consistent strategy to address Myanmar's humanitarian needs.[44] This might involve the appointment of a new special envoy, a step the US has supported. Gambari was entrusted to visit Myanmar in May 2006, to assess what might be done by the UN and the SPDC to move the country towards 'all-inclusive democracy, sustainable development and true national reconciliation'.[45] His discussions and findings are likely to influence the course of action by the UNSG and UNSC members and might also become the subject of a further briefing of the UNSC, at which the UNSG may again propose that the UNSC adopt a resolution that would avoid unambiguously locating its authority in Chapter VII, while implicitly warning that the next step for the UNSC might well be to determine that the situation constitutes a threat to international peace under Article 39. The reason for being deliberately unspecific and delaying the Article 39 determination would be to avoid a Chinese and Russian veto.

Meanwhile, in the face of a possible binding UNSC resolution, the military regime will have to reconsider whether to flout it, at the risk of enforcement action. From the perspective of Myanmar's regime it would thus probably be best if its international partners used either their 'pocket veto'[46] to keep the country off the formal agenda altogether or, if the issue is included in the agenda, to cast their veto to prevent a possible Chapter VII resolution on the situation in Myanmar from ever being passed.

Conclusion

To argue that Myanmar has not cooperated with the UN at all since 1989 is not tenable. There have, however, been obvious limits to this cooperation because the military regime has viewed its political-security imperative as incompatible with several political demands contained in UNGA and UNCHR resolutions. Cooperation with the UN has declined markedly since October 2004. In the second half of 2005, the UNSG faced increasing pressure as support grew for the UNSC to get a better grip on the situation in the country, on the grounds that Myanmar constitutes a threat to international peace and security. The SPDC's response to the UNSG's 'quasi-deadline' of mid-2006 for at least some of his appeals to be met will be carefully analysed in Washington and elsewhere. Given both the positions staked out and the dynamics of the conflict between Myanmar and the West, even a renewed release of ASSK would be inadequate to protect the SPDC from further pressure. It would be a major historical irony if Myanmar, which joined the UN to better protect itself against threats to its sovereignty and territorial integrity, were to find that preventing UNSC involvement had become its primary foreign-policy challenge.

CONCLUSION

Although faced with severe challenges both at home and internationally, Myanmar has managed to pursue a partially successful foreign policy, which has contributed to state and regime security and opened up avenues for increasing economic cooperation. Confronting a comprehensive set of economic and diplomatic sanctions by the United States and the European Union, as well as the suspension of development assistance by Japan, Myanmar's key foreign-policy success has involved exploiting opportunities to build stronger political and economic relations with its three key immediate neighbours. Relations with China, India and Thailand have not been without challenges of their own, but by 2005 all three unambiguously supported Yangon's quest for development, were interested in cooperating with the SPDC to promote regional economic integration and to address harmful transnational security challenges, and provided diplomatic support for the military regime. Myanmar's decision to participate in regional and sub-regional multilateral institutions has also yielded limited benefits (primarily diplomatic), even if intramural relations within ASEAN have become less straightforward because some members regard Myanmar as threatening Southeast Asia's collective standing. The SPDC's diplomatic efforts in early 2006 – geared towards ensuring that the UNSC does not decide formally to take issue with Myanmar – strengthened relations with China, India and Russia, and won an apparent assurance from Beijing that it would use its veto if necessary.

Myanmar's foreign policy towards the US, EU and Japan has, however, proved largely ineffective in that the regime has failed to persuade these states to modify their respective punitive stances towards the regime. By making foreign policy a function of the doggedly pursued domestic political-security imperative, the military regime has reinforced a cycle of defiance, punitive measures and resolve that pervades its relations with Washington in particular, where the regime continues to be regarded as illegitimate beyond repair. While the crackdown on ASSK and her entourage at Depayin perhaps made sense for the regime against the backdrop of an unstable domestic political situation, the military leadership may have underestimated the extent to which this move would release yet unspent political energies in the US and international activist circles to bring democracy and human rights to Myanmar. The SPDC's tough response to perceived provocations by ASSK and her domestic supporters has also played an important part in limiting support from essentially non-partisan actors: the UNSG, his special envoys and the special rapporteur of the UNCHR. Since the ouster of Khin Nyunt, Myanmar's relations with the West and ASEAN have deteriorated steadily. As David Steinberg has argued, 'Wherever the problems with compromise may lie, the military regime will be seen to be responsible.'[1]

It would be inaccurate to argue that the SPDC did not notice Myanmar's vulnerability to accusations of posing a threat to international peace and security, as is illustrated by its unequivocal reaction to rumours about nuclear cooperation with North Korea. However, the regime may have underestimated the likelihood of the US making a sustained effort to forge a multilateral strategy towards Myanmar that involves placing the country under UNSC scrutiny in light of the deterioration of its human rights and humanitarian situation and their related crossborder impact. The reason for this is not entirely clear. After all, Washington has invested considerable political capital in making the SPDC embrace a veritable political transition towards democracy, as illustrated by its vigorous opposition to the modalities of the regime's NC and its call for a genuinely substantive dialogue. Indeed, Washington must take little comfort from the thought that the SPDC could actually successfully complete its task in working out the constitution and winning acceptance for it by referendum. Such success would greatly enhance the legitimacy of the military, at the expense of the NLD. With 25% of seats to be reserved for the military in a future parliament the armed forces would also have a sufficiently strong blocking vote to prevent amendments to a constitution that seems designed to allow the present leaders to assume executive power for many years to come.

Whither Myanmar's politics and foreign policy?

The weakening position and ultimate removal of Khin Nyunt and MI in 2004 has had a palpable effect on how Myanmar has conducted its foreign relations. With Khin Nyunt went not only a national decision-maker and his team, who together constructed reasonably good working relationships with other regional and international leaders, but also the idea that taking chances both at home and abroad from a position of strength might produce positive results for the country. As Pinheiro put it, Khin Nyunt 'recognized the necessity and value of the political opposition and its potentially constructive role in the transition to democracy'.[2] For the present military leadership the lesson, now learned twice, is that the release of ASSK may not only compromise domestic stability, but is also unlikely to bring respite from external demands for political change and no substantial material benefits or recognition. Unsurprisingly, ASSK's detention under house arrest was extended in November 2005.

Irrespective of ASSK's situation, the perceived political-security imperative will remain at the heart of domestic politics for the foreseeable future. Internal stability is not guaranteed, as evidenced by a series of bomb attacks throughout the country.[3] The main reason for the continued significance of the political-security imperative, however, is that the SPDC's conflict with the ethnic minorities remains far from resolved, even though by 2004 a 'considerable degree of consensus' had emerged between non-ceasefire groups, ceasefire groups and electoral parties over the ways forward to attain national reconciliation.[4] However, a permanent ceasefire agreement has yet to be agreed between the SPDC and a number of armed groups, most notably the KNU, the Karenni National Progressive Party and the SSA-South. Yangon's relations with ceasefire groups are also volatile. Attempts since October 2004 to oblige these armed ethnic-minority groups to lay down their weapons have been resisted in several quarters, leading to violence even between the army and its 'ally', the UWSA.[5] Several ceasefire groups have signalled that they will not be disarming without adequate security guarantees.[6] One of the regime's 17 ceasefire arrangements – with the Shan State National Army (SSNA) – seems to have come undone. The reported merger of the SSNA with the SSA-South has resulted in significant military operations.

Ceasefire groups have a number of concerns beyond physical security. These include fears about the army confiscating land or being deprived of economic support and business concessions.[7] Suspicions about government intentions persist, alongside frustrations over broken promises. Some have been frustrated that their constitutional proposals have failed to elicit

a positive response from the regime and withdrawn their active cooperation.[8] The NC has also only included six out of eight legal ethnic-minority
parties.[9] In February 2005 the regime arrested Major-General Sao Hso Ten,
president of the Shan State Peace Council, an umbrella group consisting of SSA-North and SSNA, alongside other prominent Shan leaders. In
November 2005 they were convicted on charges of treason for allegedly
holding political discussions about the NC considered to be obstructing its
successful completion. Such moves have not contributed to confidence and
security-building between the regime and the ethnic groups; the potential
for more ceasefires to go awry exists, especially if armed ethnic-minority
groups believe that external assistance might be available to further their
respective causes. Conversely, the actions of the ethnic-minority groups
have done little to allay suspicions that armed groups harbour ethnic
nationalist aspirations. Even in the unlikely event of Than Shwe stepping
aside soon, it is improbable that the military regime would soon reassess
its political-security imperative.

With the political-security imperative firmly in place, Myanmar's basic
foreign-policy objectives – the defence of the country's sovereignty and
territorial integrity, the protection against political threats to the regime
and the deepening of relations with international partners willing to assist
in the country's development – will not undergo fundamental change soon.
To the extent that it is possible, the SPDC will also pursue an independent foreign policy. Whether it sees itself as being able to do so depends in
many ways on Western policy, particularly US policy towards Myanmar,
as the substance of this policy is likely to impact on the nature of Yangon's
external alignments.

Four approaches

For illustrative purposes it is possible to distinguish four possible Western
policy alternatives to dealing with the SPDC. The first involves basically
continuing to apply more or less the same type and amount of pressure to
bring about desired policy changes within Myanmar. At least two ration-
ales inform this approach. The first is that there is no reason to re-evaluate
policy towards Myanmar because the situation there has not intrinsically
changed: the regime remains in power, ASSK is again under house arrest,
human-rights violations continue and the prospects for democratisation
remain uncertain if not poor. The second rationale is that, because Myanmar
is neither an industrialised country nor subject to economic and political
sanctions from its immediate neighbours, there is little point in strengthening the existing sanctions regime. At the same time, with the West having

specified the conditions that Myanmar must fulfil for sanctions to be lifted, this approach leaves little room to change current policy, as the sanctions also serve to assuage domestic and international public opinion. In practice, this approach implies that domestic change in Myanmar would only come about if, when and as the regime wants it to happen.

The second option involves increasing the pressure on the basis that the problem with current policies is that Western efforts to punish the regime and ASEAN's engagement approach have not produced significant results. It is predicated on the notion that the objectives of political reconciliation and a transition towards democracy now need to be achieved, albeit on the basis of greater and wider efforts. Myanmar's regime is considered to be at fault for the dire economic, human-rights and humanitarian situation prevailing in the country, particularly the serious suffering of ethnic minorities, which can no longer be allowed to continue. This tougher-minded alternative favours a new multilateral approach including the ASEAN states and Myanmar's two key economic partners and political backers: China and India. The goal is to reduce considerably the regime's comfort zone. Placing Myanmar on the agenda of the UNSC for constituting a threat to peace and security and, if possible, obtaining a resolution to force the SPDC's hand would be aspects of this strategy.

The third option also begins with the premise that Western sanctions do not constitute a particularly effective foreign-policy instrument, be it to attain political concessions, national reconciliation, democratisation or rapid regime change.[10] Indeed, the argument is that negative sanctions might sustain rather than undermine military rule, not least because they provide a scapegoat for the country's economic woes. It argues that the focus in policy on Myanmar should be re-directed towards engagement, albeit on a conditional basis, in contradistinction to an insipid form of 'constructive engagement'. This involves deciding on a set of positive rather than negative sanctions. Targeted economic sanctions would be tied to measurable and verifiable progress towards the implementation of an agreed set of political reforms.[11] Benchmarks would be set by countries applying sanctions, in consultation with the UNSG, and could also be used as incentives to obtain benefits such as funding from the World Bank, IMF or ADB.[12] The approach also advises a unified approach between Western and Asian countries to reduce opportunities for the SPDC to play one country off another.[13] Another facet is for joint efforts in developing state capacity to make Myanmar's democracy work.[14]

The fourth option is, in effect, an extension of the third. Its exponents favour going 'beyond politics' and dealing with the varied structural problems that the country is facing.[15] This approach argues that Myanmar should be given unconditional international support to assist and promote conflict prevention and resolution, institution building, planning for economic development, and that these steps should be accompanied by more humanitarian aid.[16] It calls for a focus on bottom–up strategies and targeted assistance, as well as addressing the need for confidence-building in ethnic-minority areas.[17] Indeed, the key objective of such an approach is to help move the country beyond its current stagnation and the unceasing battle of political wills towards embracing a collective mentality shift that would be about learning new ways to deal with conflict.[18] The argument is, for instance, that humanitarian and longer-term development assistance to remote areas affected by armed conflict involving emerging civil society actors can be implemented in ways that address long-standing structures of violence and injustice.[19] As some argue, assistance provided to Myanmar's border regions could ultimately both lay the foundations for a more open, democratic system and address transnational security threats.[20] Advocates of this approach appreciate that such focused assistance would not yield immediate political results across the democratisation and human-rights front, but they emphasise the importance of a 'win-win situation' as a necessary underpinning for confidence-building measures and the gradual relaxation of Yangon's policies, if not the military's political-security imperative itself.

The need to foster new cooperative approaches is also emphasised by Pinheiro, who has argued that the international community cannot wait for the end of the political transition to cooperate on initiatives aimed at improving the lives of vulnerable people in Myanmar and those of Burmese refugees.[21] This position necessarily demands the recognition that, for political change to proceed, the military will remain an important stakeholder for the foreseeable future and that addressing the conflict between the Bamar majority and the ethnic minorities is the most urgent and important task. While the third and fourth approaches, in particular, are not necessarily exclusive, the second and third, which are both likely to involve the UNSG when implemented, may either be incompatible with or insufficient to induce a softening of the SPDC's perceived political-security imperative.

Western governments increasingly argue that, particularly because of the dire human-rights and humanitarian situation in Myanmar, simply maintaining the status quo is no longer tenable. However, there is no firm consensus among Western countries on an alternative approach. The EU has indicated interest in embracing some elements of the fourth approach, while maintaining a critical dialogue.[22] The US government has favoured moving to the second approach and, in 2005, began to implement it, with the apparent support of the American media and public. Meanwhile, in July 2005 the *Economist* supported the idea of rewarding the SPDC for positive steps and, hence, 'marrying' Western sanctions with Eastern engagement.[23] Such differences notwithstanding, Western policy towards Myanmar is likely to be shaped by Washington. And though the second Bush administration may still be preoccupied with developments in Iraq, Iran and North Korea, Myanmar is firmly on its radar. Washington has unambiguously indicated that it will continue to press for a transition to democracy along the lines of the second approach, while providing humanitarian assistance.[24] The political dynamics are conspicuous as illustrated by the bipartisan support in the Senate for a resolution calling on the US to lead an effort at the UNSC to pass a legally binding, non-punitive resolution immediately.[25] It is expected that the Bush administration will decide whether to reinforce its political efforts after mid-2006, once the informal deadline for the SPDC to initiate positive change as stipulated by the UNSG has passed.

It is thus important to clarify the potential issues and implications associated with intensifying pressure on Myanmar. The first is that ASSK would have to be able and willing to amend many of her positions. Though reinforcing pressure on the SPDC would be intended to undo injustice and to empower both ASSK and the NLD, Western governments should be mindful that while very much revered, ASSK and her loyal supporters are not uncontroversial within Myanmar, among the ethnic nationalities and within the exile community. Indeed, ASSK's critics from the Free Burma Coalition, who campaigned on her behalf for years for sanctions against the regime, lament her authoritarian leadership style as well as her inability to 'serve as a catalyst for change', and complain about Western governments according her 'papal infallibility'.[26] They also suggest that the NLD has failed to address adequately 'common problems' that call for shared responsibilities. They point out that ASSK and the NLD have lacked a pragmatic national reconciliation initiative, insisted on a 'misguided opposition' to economic integration of the national economy, ignored the concerns of ethnic minorities and undermined Myanmar's strategic interests.[27] Another issue concerns the capacity of the NLD. It is commonly asserted that the NLD is only a shadow of its former self.[28] Even the State Department argued only recently that 'it is difficult to assess the current institutional strength of the NLD ... the younger generation of leaders may not yet have all the necessary skills to perform to their potential'.[29] Its decision not to participate in the NC and its failure to engage in constructive politics has damaged its political prospects at least in the short term.[30] This raises important questions about how the United States government might see regime change working out in practice.

The risks of upping the pressure

Of the four policy alternatives, heightened international pressure specifically designed to haul Myanmar onto the UNSC agenda is potentially the most counter-productive, if the objective is to promote stability and a political transition without provoking developments within Myanmar and in its foreign policy that have undesirable implications. The SPDC's response to the threat of possible UNSC action underlines this. Spurred by China's alleged promise to protect Myanmar from UNSC scrutiny, the SPDC has again increased its pressure on both the NLD and ethnic minorities. The NLD's February 2006 proposal for those elected in the 1990 general elections to recognise the incumbent SPDC as a transitional government was rejected outright.[31] In April 2006, the government suggested that it had reason to ban the party by dint of its alleged ties with 'terrorists and destructive groups', prompting further party resignations. The army also engaged in its biggest offensive against the Kayin in more than a decade, causing considerable displacement among civilians and resulting in a new outflow of refugees into Thailand. The regime may believe that establishing military control over areas previously held by the KNU's armed wing could yield political advantage in the future, perhaps by accelerating the prospect of a permanent ceasefire. The SPDC may, of course, also resort to military action because it fears direct or proxy intervention on its eastern border. The internal displacements and human suffering associated with efforts to establish military control over the border region, regardless of humanitarian considerations, could generate new problems with Thailand, and add fuel to the political conflict between Myanmar and the West because events on the ground would reinforce the arguments of those who believe that the regime poses a threat to peace and security.

Within only three months of the initial briefing of the UNSC in December 2005, the SPDC had expended considerable diplomatic effort in shoring up support from Beijing, New Delhi and Moscow. Renewed diplomatic attempts by Western governments to isolate the regime or to accelerate the transition to democracy could make Yangon consolidate, if not further strengthen, relations with these three major powers. Ironically, Western governments and their partners in Asia could find that tightening the screws on Myanmar is a costly enterprise, even if the West succeeds in securing a UNSC resolution acceptable to China and Russia.

The scenario is relatively straightforward. Even if the UN is able to restart its good-offices role and initiate a new round of separate meetings with the regime and ASSK, Myanmar continues to defy external demands for a genuine tripartite dialogue. After all, standing up to external pressure is, for military leaders, a matter of personal and national pride.[32] Small concessions might perhaps be made, but Myanmar's cooperation would overall fall short of international demands and expectations. Having invested increasing amounts of moral and political capital in the 'Burma issue', the likelihood of at least the current US administration conceding to the SPDC is remote. Indeed, for the sake of its credibility, the US government would probably seek to move the conflict with Myanmar's military regime into the next round. Conditional on what other preoccupations and challenges it faces, the temptation for the Bush administration to advance its agenda by doing more to promote political change in Myanmar during the remainder of the term must, in any case, be considerable. To avoid any prospect of punitive UNSC resolutions the military junta might then calculate that it is necessary to further strengthen ties with China. This could take various forms, of course, ranging from greater efforts to satisfy Chinese requests for intensified economic and security cooperation to silently adjusting aspects of its independent foreign policy and associated principles. The only alternative to securing a Chinese veto at the UNSC would be to secure such an undertaking by Russia. Enhancing military and economic relations with Moscow will, therefore, continue to be a key foreign-policy objective. However, in view of Beijing's longstanding diplomatic support and its significance for Myanmar's economic development, the SPDC would focus on retaining China's unequivocal backing in the first instance. By implication, China's role as primary pillar in the military government's foreign policy would be reinforced, notwithstanding the counter-balancing motive against China that already informs Yangon's ties with New Delhi and Moscow.

The ASEAN countries and Japan would feel uncomfortable with this development. ASEAN admitted Myanmar in part to offer the SPDC greater freedom of manoeuvre in its foreign policy. None of the ASEAN members are keen to see Myanmar becoming more beholden to China. Beyond public castigation, ASEAN would also find it difficult to endorse practical measures to compel Myanmar to take steps that hitherto they have not expected Yangon to take, not least because this implies adding to existing stresses in relations with the SPDC regime and could undermine the ASEAN's inclusive regionalist project. Having for a long time worried about China's increasing economic presence and possible undue political influence, Tokyo too would hardly want the conflict between the Western countries and Myanmar to be addressed by the UNSC, if this resulted in a deepening of ties between the military regime and Beijing. Given its concerns about Chinese influence in Myanmar, India's government would react similarly.

Western countries bent on further confronting Myanmar and pressuring its Asian neighbours and partners in support of increased coercion without duly taking their interests into account will ultimately create friction in their relations with these countries, even if they emphasise a multilateral approach. Trying to advance the cause of freedom in Myanmar over the objections of its Southeast Asian partners has the potential to damage America's standing as a benign regional hegemon. European governments will have to ask themselves what is to be gained by straight-jacketing relations with Southeast Asia, particularly as the European Union states seemed prepared to accept that the best way of developing inter-regional relations with Southeast Asia would involve engaging and assisting Myanmar. There is even the potential for renewed transatlantic discontent in dealing with Myanmar.

Western countries do have geopolitical interests in Myanmar. In the context of the rise of China and India, their competition for influence in South Asia, a similar competition for influence among the major powers in Southeast Asia and the uncertain prospects for regional and international security, it matters whether Myanmar is strongly dependent on China for regime survival. This can only enhance Beijing's strategically important access to the Bay of Bengal, the Andaman Sea and the Indian Ocean, as well as bolster its position in continental Southeast Asia. By presenting a threat to its sovereignty and security, Western policy also has the political effect of limiting Myanmar's primary partnerships with China, India and Russia, while Yangon's relationship with ASEAN becomes less relevant for the generals. An approach perceived by Myanmar as non-hostile and constructive would instead over time make for greater balance in the regime's practice of its declared independent and active foreign policy.[33] A Myanmar government willing and better able to deal with domestic issues that give rise to transnational security challenges is generally also desirable from a Western perspective.

Yangon's foreign policy, centred as it still is on the domestic political-security imperative, may well be awkward, provocative and at times counter-productive, but it is the product of complex and deep-rooted structural beliefs and impediments. The challenge for Western governments is to work out how to balance their human-rights and humanitarian objectives with their political and security interests in the wider South and Southeast Asian region. They should recognise that some approaches to dealing with Myanmar are more likely to be successful than others in overcoming the regime's political-security imperative and its legacy. Equally, the challenge is to realise that everyone would be best served if, as Myanmar is encouraged to embrace a process of gradual political transition and democratisation, its government felt sufficiently secure in order for it to pursue the kind of responsible and balanced, independent and active foreign policy that its Southeast Asian neighbours and Japan, as well as others, favour as the wider region of East Asia undergoes important geopolitical change.

NOTES

Introduction

1 John R. Bolton, Remarks to the Press on the Situation in Burma, 16 December 2005: http://www.state.gov/p/io/rls/rm/58913.htm.

2 ASEAN, Chairman's Statement of the 11th ASEAN Summit, 'One Vision, One Identity, One Community', Kuala Lumpur, 12 December 2005: http://www.aseansec.org/18039.htm. Myanmar's seven-step roadmap focuses on the 'reconvening of the National Convention adjourned since 1996...[the] drafting of a new constitution', its 'adoption through national referendum', the 'holding of free and fair elections for Pyithu Hluttaws (legislative bodies) according to the new constitution', the 'convening of Hluttaws' and the 'building of a modern, developed and democratic nation by the state leaders of elected Hluttaws, and the government and other central organs'. See Khin Maung Win, 'Myanmar Road to Democracy: The Way Forward', Presentation to the Seminar on Understanding Myanmar, Yangon, 27–8 January 2004: http://www.mewashingtondc.com/Road_Map_Process_files/Myanmar_Road_to_Democracy_The_Way_Forward.htm. For a discussion, see Robert H. Taylor, 'Myanmar: Roadmap to Where?', in Daljit Singh and Chin Kin Wah, eds, Southeast Asian Affairs 2004 (Singapore: Institute of Southeast Asian Studies [ISEAS], 2004), pp. 171–84.

3 For assessments of Myanmar's human rights situation, see Human Rights Watch Asia: http://hrw.org/doc/?t=asia&c=burma.

4 The work of the ICRC is on-going. The ICRC delegation in Myanmar employs 60 expatriates and 298 national staff in its Yangon head office and 5 sub-delegations (Taunggyi, Kyaing Tong, Mandalay, Mawlamyine and Hpa-An). However, since the end of 2005 the ICRC has not conducted detention visits in response to the military's decision to challenge what the ICRC regards as standard working modalities.

5 Marwaan Macan-Markar, 'AI visit to Burma: Seeks release of political prisoners', Inter Press Service, 14 February 2003.

Chapter One

1 Mary P. Callahan, Making Enemies: War and State Building in Burma (Ithaca, NY: Cornell University Press, 2003).

2 The SPDC is, in effect, the reconstituted SLORC, although only the chairman, vice-chairman and the two SLORC secretaries survived the change to the ruling echelon of the military regime in 1997.

3 As of February 2005, the SPDC had 12 members comprising the chairman and

commander-in-chief of defence services; the vice-chairman and deputy commander-in-chief of defence services; secretary-1 (ranked fifth); and nine members, including the joint chief of staff of the army, navy and air force (ranked third); the prime minister (ranked fourth); the quartermaster general; the chief of armed forces training; the chief of military ordnance; and the chiefs of the bureaux of special operations: http://www.irrawaddy.org/aviewer.asp?a=454&z=14.

4   For the official version of the background to Khin Nyunt's dismissal, see *Explanations given by Member of SPDC General Thura Shwe Mann and Prime Minister Lt. General Soe Win*, 24 October 2004 and *Explanation by Secretary-1, Lt. General Thein Sein* on October 22, 2004. An alternative explanation can be found in Kyaw Yin Hlaing, 'Myanmar in 2004: Why Military Rule Continues', in Singh and Wah, eds, *Southeast Asian Affairs 2005* (Singapore: ISEAS, 2005), pp. 232–8.

5   John H. Badgley, 'Strategic Interests in Myanmar', in Badgley, ed., 'Reconciling Burma/Myanmar: Essays on U.S. Relations with Burma', *NBR Analysis*, vol. 15, no. 1, March 2004, p. 14.

6   Tin Maung Maung Than, 'Myanmar: Military in Charge', in John Funston, ed., *Government and Politics in Southeast Asia* (Singapore: ISEAS, 2001), p. 218.

7   Andrew Selth, *Burma's Armed Forces: Power Without Glory* (Norwalk, CT: EastBridge, 2002), p. 113. A similar view is taken in International Crisis Group (ICG), *Myanmar: The Military Regime's View of the World*, ICG Asia Report, no. 28, 7 December 2001, p. 8: http://www.crisisgroup.org/home/index.cfm?id=1531&l=1.

8   In Myanmar, the politics of survival are associated with the practice of the guiding principles of the three *ma: ma loke* (not doing any work), *ma-shote* (not getting involved in any complication) and *ma-pyoke* (not getting dismissed). See Kyaw Yin Hlaing, 'Reconsidering the failure of the Burma Socialist Programme Party government to eradicate internal economic impediments', *South East Asia Research*, vol. 11, no. 1, March 2003, p. 35.

9   The five principles are: (i) mutual respect of each other's territorial integrity and sovereignty; (ii) mutual non-aggression; (iii) mutual non-interference in each other's internal affairs; (iv) equality and mutual benefit; and (v) peaceful coexistence.

10 See 'Independent and Active Foreign Policy', Myanmar Ministry of Foreign Affairs: http://www.mofa.gov.mm/foreignpolicy/foreignpolicyview2.html; Khin Maung Win, 'Foreign Policy of Myanmar: A Brief Overview', in Myanmar Ministry of Foreign Affairs, *Towards Democracy by Home Grown Process* (Yangon: Myanmar Ministry of Foreign Affairs, 2004), pp. 257–8; Thaung Tun, 'Priorities in Myanmar Foreign Policy', 10 August 2004: http://www.asiantribune.com/show_article.php?id=1688; William C. Johnstone, *Burma's Foreign Policy: a Study in Neutralism* (Cambridge, MA: Harvard University Press, 1963); Chi-shad Liang, *Burma's Foreign Relations: Neutralism in Theory and Practice* (Boulder, CO: Praeger, 1990), pp. 62–3. For Burma's foreign policy before Ne Win's 1962 takeover, see Johnstone, *Burma's Foreign Policy*.

11 Aung-Thwin, '1948 and Burma's Myth of Independence', in Josef Silverstein, ed., *Independent Burma at Forty Years: Six Assessments* (Ithaca, NY: Cornell University Southeast Asia Program, 1989), pp. 19–34.

12 Aung-Thwin, '1948 and Burma's Myth of Independence', p. 25.

13 For the themes addressed in this paragraph, see Martin Smith, *Burma: Insurgency and the Politics of Ethnicity* (London: Zed Books, 2006 [updated edn]); Bertil Lintner, *Burma in Revolt: Opium and Insurgency since 1948* (Chiang Mai: Silkworm Books, 1999); Robert H. Taylor, *The State in Burma* (London: C.Hurst, 1987); Callahan, *Making Enemies*; Ashley South, *Mon Nationalism and Civil War in Burma: The Golden Sheldrake* (London: Routledge, 2003). Also see Chao Tzang Yawnghe, 'Burma: The Depoliticization

of the Political', in Muthiah Alagappa, ed., *Political Legitimacy in Southeast Asia: the Quest for Moral Authority* (Stanford, CA: Stanford University Press, 1995), pp. 170–92, and his earlier 'The Burman Military: Holding the country together?' in Silverstein, ed., *Independent Burma at Forty Years*, pp. 81–101.

14 Taylor, 'Burma: Political Leadership, Security Perceptions and Policies' in Mohammed Ayoob and Chai-Anan Samudavanija, eds, *Leadership Perceptions and National Security: The Southeast Asian Experience* (Singapore: ISEAS, 1989), pp. 205–223.

15 Badgley, 'The Foreign Policy of Burma' in David Wurfel and Bruce Burton, eds, *The Political Economy of Foreign Policy in Southeast Asia* (Basingstoke: Palgrave Macmillan, 1990), pp. 204–18.

16 For an overview, see ICG, *Myanmar Backgrounder: Ethnic Minority Politics*, ICG Asia Report, no. 52, 7 May 2003, pp. 28–9: http://www.crisisgroup.org/home/index.cfm?id=1528&l=1.

17 The four political objectives are: (1) stability of the state, community peace and tranquillity, prevalence of law and order; (2) national reconsolidation; (3) emergence of a new enduring State Constitution; (4) building of a new modern developed nation in accord with the new State Constitution. The four economic objectives are: (1) development of agriculture as the base and all round development of other sectors of the economy; (2) proper evolution of the market-oriented economic system; (3) development of the economy inviting participation in terms of technical know-how and investments from sources inside the country and abroad; and (4) the initiative to shape the national economy must be kept in the hands of the state and the national peoples. The four social objectives are: (1) the uplift of the morale and morality of the entire nation; (2) the uplift of national prestige and integrity, and the preservation and safeguarding of cultural heritage and national character; (3) the uplift of dynamism of patriotic spirit; and

(4) the uplift of health, fitness and education standards of the entire nation.

18 Tin Maung Maung Than, 'Myanmar: Preoccupation with Regime Survival, National Unity and Stability' in Muthiah Alagappa, ed., *Asian Security Practice: Material and Ideational Influences* (Stanford: Stanford University Press, 1998), p. 394.

19 See Smith, 'Ethnic Politics and Regional Development in Myanmar: The Need for New Approaches', in Kyaw Yin Hlaing, Taylor, Tin Maung Maung Than, eds, *Myanmar: Beyond Politics to Societal Imperatives* (Singapore: ISEAS, 2005), pp. 70–71.

20 For an overview see ICG, *Myanmar Backgrounder: Ethnic Minority Politics*.

21 Soe Mya Kyaw, 'Executive Structure and Essence of the Future State', *New Light of Myanmar*, 30 January 2006, pp. 8–9.

22 Maung Cedana, 'Wearing the same old nether garment', *New Light of Myanmar*, 7 April 2006, pp. 8–9.

23 Callahan, 'Democracy in Burma: The Lessons of History', *NBR Analysis*, vol. 9, no. 3, May 1998, p. 18.

24 *Ibid.*, p. 17. For relevant studies and insights, see Christina Fink, *Living in Silence: Burma under Military Rule* (London: Zed Books, 2001); Monique Skidmore, *Karaoke Fascism: Burma and the Politics of Fear* (Philadelphia, PA: University of Pennsylvannia Press, 2004); Hazel Lang, *Fear and Sanctuary: Burmese Refugees in Thailand* (Ithaca, NY: Cornell Southeast Asia Program Publications, 2002).

25 J.S. Furnivall, *Colonial Policy and Practice: a Comparative Study of Burma and Netherlands India* (Cambridge: Cambridge University Press, 1948); Thant Myint-U, *The Making of Modern Burma* (Cambridge: Cambridge University Press, 2000).

26 On nationalism in Myanmar see Mikael Gravers, 'Nationalism as Political Paranoia in Burma: An Essay on the Historical Practice of Power', *NIAS Reports*, no. 11 (Copenhagen: Nordic Institute of Asian Studies, 1993).

27 ICG, *Myanmar: the Military Regime's View of the World*, p. 5.

28 Major General Moe Hein, National Defence College, Yangon, 'Security Challenges of the 21st Century: A Regional/National Perspective', Paper presented to the 8th ARF Heads of Defence Colleges Meeting, Singapore, September 2004: http://www.mindef.gov.sg/8arfmeet/presentations/myanmar_presentation.pdf.

29 See Maung Aung Myoe, *Military Doctrine and Strategy in Myanmar: A Historical Perspective*, Working Paper no. 339 (Canberra: Strategic and Defence Studies Centre, Australian National University, 1999), pp. 7–13; Smith, *Burma: Insurgency and the Politics of Ethnicity*.

30 See, however, Samuel Blythe, 'Myanmar's junta fears US invasion', *Asia Times*, 28 April 2006: http://www.atimes.com/atimes/Southeast_Asia/HD28Ae03.html.

31 Myanmar's military has been quietly upgrading its military capability. Selth, *Burma's Secret Military Partners*, Canberra Papers on Strategy and Defence, no. 136 (Canberra: Strategic and Defence Studies Centre, Australian National University, 2000).

32 See Maung Maung Myoe, *Military Doctrine and Strategy in Myanmar*, p. 22.

33 Thaung Tun, 'Priorities in Myanmar Foreign Policy', 10 August 2004, p. 4.

34 Tin Maung Maung Than, 'Myanmar: Preoccupation with Regime Survival, National Unity and Stability', p. 404.

35 Major General Moe Hein, 'Security Challenges of the 21st Century: A Regional/National Perspective'.

36 For a review of Myanmar's political economy see Myat Thein, *Economic Development of Myanmar* (Singapore: ISEAS, 2004). Also see David I. Steinberg, 'Myanmar: The Roots of Economic Malaise' in *Myanmar: Beyond Politics to Societal Imperatives*, pp. 86–116.

37 J.F. Guyot, 'Burma in 1988: Perestroika with a military face', *Southeast Asian Affairs 1989* (Singapore: ISEAS, 1989), p. 113.

38 See Helen James, 'Myanmar's International Relations Strategy: The Search for Security', *Contemporary Southeast Asia*, vol. 26, no. 3, December 2004, pp. 530–53.

39 Stefan Collignon, 'Human Rights and the Economy in Burma' in Taylor, ed., *Burma: Political Economy under Military Rule* (London: C.Hurst, 2001), p. 83. Also see the discussion in Juliane Schober, 'Buddhist Visions of Moral Authority and Modernity in Burma', in Monique Skidmore, ed., *Burma at the Turn of the 21st Century* (Honolulu: University of Hawai'i Press, 2005), pp. 113–32; and Zarni and May Oo, Free Burma Coalition, *Common Problems, Shared Responsibilities: Citizens' Quest for National Reconciliation in Burma/Myanmar*, October 2004, pp. 66–70: http://www.freeburmacoalition.org/executive%20summary%20Free%20Burma%20Coalition%20report.pdf. For a different, but also common, view see Chao Tzang Yawnghe, 'Burma: The Depoliticization of the Political'.

40 The five unified eras comprise those of the great Burman monarchs Anawrahta, Bayinnaung and Alaungphaya. The fourth is Aung San and Panglong 1947 and the fifth is the present era. See Smith, *Burma: Insurgency and Politics of Ethnicity*, p. 426.

41 See for example Taylor, 'The Outlook for Myanmar and its Role in the Region', Paper given at the ISEAS 2005, Regional Outlook Forum, Shangri-La Hotel, Singapore, 6 January 2005: http://www.iseas.edu.sg/22005.pdf.

42 Mya Maung, 'The Burma Road to the Past', *Asian Survey*, vol. 39, no. 2, March/April 1999, p. 267. For an account of the role of Buddhist discourse in Myanmar's politics see Gustaaf Houtman, *Mental Culture in Burmese Crisis Politics: Aung San Suu Kyi and the National League for Democracy* (Tokyo: Institute for the Study of Languages and Culture of Asia and Africa, Tokyo University of Foreign Studies, 1999).

43 Günter Siemers, 'Suu Kyi in Myanmar: Von Konfrontation zu Kollision?', *Südostasien aktuell*, September 1998, pp. 384–402.

44 See Embassy of the Union of Myanmar in Japan, http://www.myanmar-embassy-

tokyo.net/about.html. - Different figures are available for some border lengths, see CIA, *The World Factbook*, 'Burma': http://www.cia.gov/cia/publications/factbook/geos/bm.html. On border lengths and Myanmar's geographical setting, see also Selth, *Burma's Armed Forces*, pp. 3–7.

45 Selth, *Burma's Armed Forces*, pp. 13–15.

46 J. Mohan Malik, 'Burma's Role in Regional Security: Pawn or Pivot?' in Robert I. Rotberg, ed., *Burma: Prospects for a Democratic Future* (Washington DC: Brookings, 1998), pp. 109–34. On China–India relations more generally, see Waheguru Pal Singh Sidhu and Jing-dong Yuan, *China and India: Cooperation or Conflict?* (Boulder, CO: Lynne Rienner, 2003).

47 Bruce Hawke, 'How Much does Rangoon get from the Gas', *The Irrawaddy* (Thailand), November 2004, vol. 12, no. 10, p. 11. The Yadana site has been producing since 1988, while Yetagun started production in 2000. Also see Tin Maung Maung Than, 'Myanmar's Energy Sector: Banking on Natural Gas' in *Southeast Asian Affairs 2005*, pp. 257–89.

48 Bhutan and Nepal joined in 2004.

49 See Thaung Tun, 'Priorities in Myanmar Foreign Policy', 10 August 2004.

Chapter Two

1 Chi-shad Liang, 'Burma's Relations with the People's Republic of China: from delicate friendship to genuine co-operation' in Peter Carey, ed., *Burma: The Challenge of Change in a Divided Society* (Basingstoke: Palgrave Macmillan, 1997), pp. 71–93.

2 Tin Maung Maung Than, 'Myanmar and China: A Special Relationship?', in Singh and Wah, eds, *Southeast Asian Affairs 2003* (Singapore: ISEAS, 2003), p. 197.

3 See S.D. Muni, *China's Strategic Engagement with the New ASEAN: An Exploratory Study of China's Post-Cold War Political, Strategic and Economic Relations with Myanmar, Laos, Cambodia and Vietnam*, IDSS Monograph no. 2 (Singapore: Institute of Defence and Strategic Studies, Nanyang Technological University [IDSS], 2002), pp. 77–80; Tin Maung Maung Than, 'Myanmar and China: A Special Relationship?'; Selth, *Burma's Armed Forces*.

4 Selth, *Burma's Armed Forces*, p. 119. See the 1995 paper by Yossef Bodansky, 'Beijing's Surge for the Strait of Malacca': http://www.freeman.org/m_online/bodansky/beijing.htm.

5 'Desmond Ball Unbound: Interview with Desmond Ball', *The Irrawaddy*, vol. 12, no. 6, June 2004.

6 See Desmond Ball, 'SIGINT strengths form a vital part of Burma's military muscle', *Jane's Intelligence Review*, vol. 10, no. 3, 1 March 1998: http://www.burma-fund.org/Pathfinders/Research_Library/Military/Signals.htm.

7 Selth, *Burma's Armed Forces*, p. 119.

8 Selth, *Burma's China Connection and the Indian Ocean Region*, Working Paper no. 377 (Canberra: Strategic and Defence Studies Centre, Australian National University, 2003), p. 6.

9 See, for example, C.S. Kuppuswamy, 'Myanmar–China Cooperation: Its Implications for India', 3 February 2003, South Asia Analysis Group, Paper no. 596: http://www.saag.org/papers6/paper596.html.

10 Bill Gertz, 'China builds up strategic sea lanes', *Washington Times*, 18 January 2005: http://www.washtimes.com/national/20050117-115550-1929r.htm.

11 Selth, *Burma's Secret Military Partners*.

12 William Ashton, 'The Arms Keep Coming – But Who Pays?', *The Irrawaddy*, vol. 12, no. 6, June 2004, pp. 18–19.

13 Ashton, 'The Arms Keep Coming – But Who Pays?'; arms imports in recent years have also been lower than in the early 1990s. According to SIPRI, Myanmar's estimated arms expenditure in the 2000–04 period was US$447m (it was US$1m in 2000, US$130m in 2001, US$198m in 2002,

US$13m in 2003 and US$65m in 2004): http://www.sipri.org/contents/armstrad/at_data.html.

14 Selth, *Burma's Armed Forces*, p. 192.

15 Steinberg, 'Myanmar: Regional Relationships and Internal Concerns' in Derek da Cunha, ed., *Southeast Asian Affairs 1998* (Singapore: ISEAS, 1998), p. 182.

16 See Tin Maung Maung Than and Mya Than, 'Myanmar: Economic Growth and Political Constraints' in Singh, ed., *Southeast Asian Affairs 1997* (Singapore: ISEAS, 1997), p. 229.

17 The text is available at the website of the Chinese Ministry of Foreign Affairs: http://www.fmprc.gov.cn/eng/wjb/zzjg/yzs/gjlb/2747/default.htm.

18 On China's strategy and policies towards Southeast Asia, see Muni, *China's Strategic Engagement with the New ASEAN*; see also Haacke, 'Seeking Influence: China's Diplomacy towards ASEAN after the Asian Crisis', *Asian Perspective*, vol. 26, no. 4, 2002, pp. 13–52, and the contributions in Ho Khai Leong and Samuel C.Y. Ku, eds, *China and Southeast Asia: Global Changes and Regional Challenges* (Singapore: ISEAS, 2005).

19 Chinese Ministry of Foreign Affairs, 'Bilateral Relations [with Myanmar]'.

20 See 'Chinese Companies Building Hydropower Projects in Myanmar', *Xinhua News Agency*, 2 September 2005: http://www.china.org.cn/english/environment/140671.htm.

21 'Shweli Hydel Power Project', 19 August 2003, Myanmar Ministry of Foreign Affairs: http://www.mofa.gov.mm/news/aug19_tue_shweli.html. For an overview of dam-building activities, see Yuki Akimoto, 'Hydro-powering the Regime', *The Irrawaddy*, vol. 12, no. 6, June 2004.

22 A full list of agreements is available from the Myanmar Ministry of Foreign Affairs: http://www.mofa.gov.mm/news/feb29_mon_04_7.html.

23 The stake now belongs to Chevron which acquired Unocal in 2005.

24 'Deep Water Port for Ramree Island', *The Irrawaddy*, vol. 13, no. 1, January 2005, p. 5.

25 Rodney Tasker and Bertil Lintner, 'Danger: Road Works Ahead', *Far Eastern Economic Review*, 21 December 2000, pp. 26–7.

26 Pan Qi, 'Opening the Southwest: An Expert Opinion', *Beijing Review*, vol. 28, no. 35, 2 September 1985, pp. 22–3.

27 John W. Garver, 'Development of China's Overland Transportation Links with Central, South-west and South Asia', *China Quarterly*, no. 185, March 2006, p. 12.

28 Marwaan Macan-Markar, 'Myanmar gets a friend, China gets its forests', *Asia Times*, 20 October 2005: http://www.atimes.com/atimes/Southeast_Asia/GJ20Ae01.html.

29 Aung Zaw, 'Hijacked: A political breakthrough', *Bangkok Post*, 16 May 2006.

30 'Agreements inked with Myanmar', *China Daily*, 13 July 2004: http://www.chinadaily.com.cn/english/doc/2004-07/13/content_347699.htm.

31 'Premier Wen Jiabao holds talks with Prime Minister of Myanmar Soe Win', Foreign Ministry of the People's Republic of China, 14 February 2006: http://www.fmprc.gov.cn/eng/wjb/zzjg/yzs/gjlb/2747/2749/t235759.htm.

32 Thet Kaing, 'China move welcomed on precursor chemicals', *The Myanmar Times*, 29 August–4 September 2005, p. 1.

33 Pierre-Arnaud Chouvy, 'The *yaa baa* phenomenon in Mainland Southeast Asia', *Harvard Asia Pacific Review*, vol. 8, no. 2, Fall 2005, pp. 19–22: http://www.pa-chouvy.org/Chouvy-HarvardAsiaPacificReview-2005-YaaBaaSoutheastAsia.html.

34 For an official overview of visits by military delegations, see 'Relationship between China People's Liberation Army and Myanmar Defense Services', Embassy of the People's Republic of China in the Union of Myanmar: http://wcm.fmprc.gov.cn/ce/cemm/eng/zt/zmjjqd/ljjwjk/t198672.htm.

35 As regards GMS cooperation, for example, Myanmar finds itself in the unfortunate position of being the only participating

country to which financial assistance is not provided by the Asian Development Bank. Accordingly, the GMS cooperation Myanmar pursues looks more like bilateral cooperation with China.

[36] Seth Mydans, 'China woos Myanmar as ASEAN seeks to deal with its leaders', *International Herald Tribune*, 29 July 2005.

[37] Larry Jagan, 'China's uneasy alliance with Myanmar', *Asia Times*, 24 February 2006.

[38] Robert B. Zoellick, Deputy Secretary of State, 'Whither China: From Membership to Responsibility?' Remarks to National Committee on US–China Relations, New York City, 21 September 2005: http://www. state.gov/s/d/rem/53682.htm. For a discussion, see the contributions to 'Whither US–China Relations?', *NBR Analysis*, vol.16, no. 4, December 2005.

[39] B. Pakem, *India–Burma Relations* (New Delhi: Omsons Publications, 1992), p. 219.

[40] Afterwards Soe Myint became the publisher of Mizzima News Group in New Delhi.

[41] On Indian foreign policy after the Cold War, see Baldev Raj Nayar and T.V. Paul, *India in the World Order: Searching for Major-Power Status* (Cambridge: Cambridge University Press, 2003), chapter six. On the Look East Policy, see Faizal Yahya, 'India and Southeast Asia: Revisited', *Contemporary Southeast Asia*, vol. 25, no. 1, April 2003, pp. 81–3.

[42] Renaud Egreteau, *Wooing the Generals: India's New Burma Policy* (New Delhi: Authorspress, 2003), pp. 135–6.

[43] For an overview of important visits by both sides, see *India–Myanmar Relations: Recent Highlights* (Yangon: Embassy of the Republic of India, 2005).

[44] The Myanmar naval chief was the first in his position to visit India in November 1999, laying the foundations for closer interaction between the two navies. Indian Chief of Army Staff General V.P. Malik paid a visit to Myanmar in July 2000, while Indian Chief of Naval Staff Admiral Sushil Kumar visited Myanmar in January 2001. In return, Commander-in-Chief Myanmar Navy Vice-Admiral Kyi Min visited India in November 2001 and Commander-in-Chief Myanmar Air Force Major-General Myat Hein visited India in late August to early September 2003. Indian Chief of Naval Staff Admiral Madhvendra Singh paid a visit to Yangon in September 2003, allegedly to discuss access to Myanmar's ports. More recently, the Indian Army Chiefs visited Myanmar in November 2005, followed by the visit of India's Chief of Naval Staff Admiral Arun Prakash in January 2006. In February 2005 the Myanmar Chief of Naval Staff Vice Admiral Soe Thein visited India.

[45] *India–Myanmar Relations: Recent Highlights*, p. 27

[46] Egreteau, *Wooing the Generals*, pp. 103–6, 109–12.

[47] 'Prime Minister Khin Nyunt inspects development tasks in Dawei, Kawthoung', *New Light of Myanmar*, 15 January 2004, p. 1. See also Ramtanu Maitra, 'The energy ties that bind India, China', *Asia Times*, 12 April 2005: http://www.atimes.com/ atimes/South_Asia/GD12Df03.html.

[48] For an overview see Tin Maung Maung Than, 'Myanmar's Energy Sector: Banking on Natural Gas'.

[49] 'B'desh delay may cost India gas from Myanmar', *Times of India*, 11 January 2006: http://timesofindia.indiatimes. com/articleshow/1367073.cms. See also Anand Kumar, 'Myanmar–PetroChina Agreement: A Setback to India's Quest for Energy Security', *South Asia Analysis Group*, paper no. 1681, 19 January 2006: http://www.saag.org/ %5Cpapers17%5Cpaper1681.html.

[50] Shiv Aroor, 'Fleet expansion in mind, Myanmar looks to India for expertise', *Indian Express*, 13 January 2006: http:// www.indianexpress.com/full_story. php?content_id=85841.

[51] Shiv Aroor, 'Navy deal with Myanmar hits UK hurdle', *Indian Express*, 24 January 2006: http://www.defenceindia.com/23- jan-2k6/news18.html.

[52] Egreteau, 'India courts a junta', *Asia Times*, 20 September 2003: http://www.

atimes.com/atimes/South_Asia/EI2oDfo8.
html.

53   See 'Joint Statement issued on the occa-
     sion of the State Visit of HE Senior
     General Than Shwe, Chairman of the
     SPDC of the Union of Myanmar to India
     (25–29 October 2004)': http://www.indi-
     aembassy.net.mm/cooperation/joint_
     statement.asp.

54   '15 Myanmarese soldiers killed: Naga
     rebels', Times of India, 14 January 2006:
     http://timesofindia.indiatimes.com/arti-
     cleshow/1371936.cms.

55   'A Naga Ultimatum: Separatist leader sets
     terms for peace with India', The Irrawaddy,
     vol. 14, no. 1, January 2006, pp. 24–5.

56   Subir Bhaumik, 'India's Balancing Act', The
     Irrawaddy, vol. 14, no. 4, April 2006, p. 13.

57   Embassy of India, Yangon, India News,
     Press Release 3/2005, 25 March 2005:
     http://www.indiaembassy.net.mm/infor-
     mation/3_2005.asp.

58   Ramtanu Maitra, 'India bids to rule the
     waves: from the Bay of Bengal to the
     Malacca Strait', Asia Times, 19 October 2005:
     http://japanfocus.org/article.asp?id=424.

Chapter Three

1   Leszek   Buszynski,   'Thailand   and
     Myanmar: the perils of "constructive"
     engagement', Pacific Review, vol. 11, no. 2,
     1998, pp. 295–6.

2   It is often erroneously suggested that
     ASEAN is still pursuing a policy 'con-
     structive engagement' even today. From
     ASEAN's point of view, constructive
     engagement refers to the engagement by
     ASEAN of an outsider and in line with this
     view, the use of the term after Myanmar
     won membership in 1997 would be inac-
     curate. The term is not, therefore, part of
     the formal language of ASEAN.

3   Buszynski, 'Thailand and Myanmar', pp.
     293–5.

4   Silverstein, 'Burma in an international
     perspective', Asian Survey, vol. 32, no. 10,
     October 1992, p. 958.

5   Silverstein, 'Burma and the World' in
     Taylor, ed., Burma: Political Economy under
     Military Rule (London: C. Hurst, 2001),
     pp. 129–30.

6   Shaun Narine, Explaining ASEAN:
     Regionalism in Southeast Asia (Boulder,
     CO: Lynne Rienner, 2002), p. 116. On the
     background to US Burma policy see also
     Leon T. Hadar, 'Burma: US Foreign Policy
     as a Morality Play', Journal of International
     Affairs, vol. 54, no. 2, Spring 2001, pp.
     411–26.

7   In the event, this was postponed due to
     events in Cambodia in early July 1997.

8   Opening Statement by HE U Ohn Gyaw,
     30th AMM, 24–5 July 1997, Subang Jaya:
     http://www.aseansec.org/4000.htm.

9   See Declaration of ASEAN Concord II
     (Bali Concord II), Bali, 7 October 2003:
     http://www.aseansec.org/15159.htm.

10   This should not be a surprise insofar as
     Myanmar is committed to a 'discipline-
     flourishing' democratic system. The
     official evaluation of the Bali Summit is
     contained in 'Prime Minister addresses
     ASEAN Steering Committee Meeting
     No 2/2003', New Light of Myanmar, 25
     October 2003: http://www.myanmar.gov.
     mm/NLM-2003/enlm/Oct25_h4.html.

11   At the time of writing, Myanmar ISIS was
     not a member of ASEAN-ISIS.

12   Mya Than, Myanmar in ASEAN: Regional
     Cooperation Experience (Singapore: ISEAS,
     2005), p. 109.

13   Steinberg, 'Myanmar: The Roots of
     Economic Malaise', in Kyaw Yin Hlaing,
     Taylor, Tin Maung Maung Than, eds,
     Myanmar: Beyond Politics to Societal
     Imperatives, pp. 86–116.

14   For a critical perspective see Bruce Hawke,
     'The Burma–Thailand Gas Debacle', The
     Irrawaddy, vol. 12, no. 10, November 2004,
     pp. 8–10.

15   Mya Than, Myanmar in ASEAN, p. 94.

16   China nevertheless remains Myanmar's
     biggest import partner by far, although
     Thailand is its most important trade

partner. See European Union, DG Trade, EU Bilateral Trade and Trade with the World: Myanmar, 9 March 2006: http://trade.ec.europa.eu/doclib/docs/2006/may/tradoc_113423.pdf.

[17] The IAI Work Plan for Cambodia, Laos, Myanmar, Vietnam (CLMV) focuses on the priority areas of Infrastructure Development (Transport and Energy), Human Resource Development (Public Sector Capacity Building, Labour and Employment, and Higher Education), Information and Communications Technology and Promoting Regional Economic Integration (Trade in Goods and Services, Customs, Standards and Investments) in the CLMV countries.

[18] Progress of IAI Work Plan: Status Update (as of 10 February 2006): www.aseansec.org/14013.htm.

[19] For the details and terms of reference of the ASEAN Development Fund see: http://www.aseansec.org/17577.htm.

[20] Also see Myanmar Information Committee, Yangon, Information Sheet no. C-2795 (I/L), 10 October 2003:http://www.mewashingtondc.com/Myanmar_Welcomes_Support_of_Asean_in_Building_Democracy.htm.

[21] Haacke, 'The concept of flexible engagement and the practice of enhanced interaction: intramural challenges to the "ASEAN way"', Pacific Review, vol. 12, no. 4, 1999, pp. 581–611.

[22] Statement by HE U Win Aung at the 32nd AMM, 23–4 July 1999, Singapore: www.aseansec.org/3834.htm.

[23] Maung Aung Myoe, Neither Friend nor Foe: Myanmar's Relations with Thailand Since 1988, A View from Yangon, IDSS Monograph no.1 (Singapore: IDSS, 2002), p. 14.

[24] See Smith, Burma: Insurgency and the Politics of Ethnicity, pp. 447–8 and Lintner, Burma in Revolt. For the officially sanctioned account, see Maung Pho Shoke, Why Did U Khun Sa's MTA Exchange Arms for Peace? (Yangon: U Aung Zaw, 1999) and Yan Nyein Aye, Endeavours of Myanmar Armed Forces Government for National Reconsolidation (Yangon: U Aung Zaw, 1999).

[25] 'Myanmar: Spannungen mit Thailand', Südostasien aktuell, March 2001, p. 141.

[26] Maung Aung Myoe, Neither Friend nor Foe, pp. 121–2. See also Tekkatho Myat Thu, 'Trouble-maker opium insurgents at border', in Waiting For Long...Didn't Say and Special Articles (Yangon: Guardian Press, 2001), pp. 1–12.

[27] Maung Aung Myoe, Neither Friend nor Foe, p. 47.

[28] 'Invitation to a Border Skirmish', Far Eastern Economic Review, 22 February 2001, p. 10.

[29] Aung Zaw, 'Tangled Ties', The Irrawaddy, vol. 8, no. 7, July 2000: http://www.irrawaddy.org/database/2000/vol8.7/specialreoprt.htm.

[30] For details see Desmond Ball, Security Developments in the Thailand–Burma Borderlands, Working Paper no. 9, (Sydney: Australian Mekong Resource Centre, University of Sydney, October 2003).

[31] Maung Aung Myoe, Neither Friend nor Foe, p. 18.

[32] 'Myanmar: Besuch von Thailands Premier Thaksin klärt Misstimmung', Südostasien aktuell, July 2001, p. 360. Myanmar state media had previously suggested that the revered Thai King Maha Mongkut 'gave away the country to keep his throne'.

[33] Tasker and Lintner, 'Nasty Job for Task Force 399', Far Eastern Economic Review, 19 April 2001, p. 25.

[34] 'Burmese Refugees Face Forced Return', Far Eastern Economic Review, 6 September 2001, p. 10.

[35] Tasker, 'The Premier's Invisible Hand', Far Eastern Economic Review, 10 October 2002, pp. 22–3.

[36] Ball, Security Developments in the Thailand–Burma Borderlands, p. 17.

[37] See Mae Fah Luang Foundation, Doi Tung Development Project International Cooperation Programme: Project Myanmar; on recent problems with this project, see Michael Black and Roland Fields, 'Access Denied', The Irrawaddy, vol. 14, no. 4, April 2006, p. 15.

38 'Burma's Generals Warm to Thais', *Far Eastern Economic Review*, 13 February 2003, p. 9.

39 See Aung Lwin Oo, 'Limbo Land', *The Irrawaddy*, vol. 13, no. 7, July 2005, p. 14. Also see Human Rights Watch, *Out of Sight, Out of Mind: Thai Policy toward Burmese Refugees* (New York: Human Rights Watch, February 2004): http://hrw.org/reports/2004/thailand0204/.

40 Thailand has since agreed to the resettlement of refugees in third countries.

41 'Speech by HE Thaksin Shinawatra at the Luncheon Hosted in Honour of HE General Khin Nyunt, Prime Minister of the Union of Myanmar at Government House, 4 June 2004': http://www.thaigov.go.th/news/speech/thaksin/sp04Jun04.htm.

42 'Burma–Thai Trade Reaches $2.26 billion', *The Irrawaddy*, vol. 14, no. 1, January 2006, p. 9.

43 This incident involved a bloody encounter when the motorcade in which ASSK travelled on 30 May near the town of Depayin in Sagaing Division was attacked by anti-NLD protestors, leading to the death of at least four people. ASSK was subsequently taken into 'protective custody'.

44 See Haacke, '"Enhanced Interaction" with Myanmar and the Project of a Security Community: Is ASEAN Refining or Breaking with its Diplomatic and Security Culture?', *Contemporary Southeast Asia*, vol. 27, no. 2, August 2005, pp. 207–10.

45 Larry Jagan, 'Burma on diplomatic offensive, little effect so far', *Asia Times*, 8 July 2003: http://www.atimes.com/atimes/Southeast_Asia/EG08Ae01.html.

46 Other scheduled visits were to Japan, China, India and Bangladesh.

47 'Senior General Than Shwe Says Suu Kyi Planned Violent Overthrow – FT', reprinted in *Burma Today News*: http://www.burmatoday.net/burmatoday2003/2003/07/030712_financialtimes.htm.

48 Quoted in 'Yangon condemns pressure to free Suu Kyi', *The Straits Times*, 7 July 2003.

49 Only at the 2005 summit did ASEAN leaders decide to draft an ASEAN charter.

50 Supalak Ganjanakhundee, 'Friendly approach to continue', *The Nation*, 21 July 2003.

51 Win Aung, 'Don't push Myanmar back into the shell', *The Straits Times*, 25 July 2003.

52 'Suu Kyi "case" solved by October', BBC News Online, 30 July 2003: http://news.bbc.co.uk/2/hi/asia-pacific/3105671.stm.

53 Jagan, 'Seeking a way out for Rangoon: Roadmap to Democracy', *Bangkok Post*, 9 August 2003.

54 Jagan, 'Seeking a way out for Rangoon'; 'Mapping the Road to Reconciliation: An interview with Kobsak Chutikil', *The Irrawaddy*, 5 August 2003: www.irrawaddy.org/news/2003/aug04.html.

55 Khin Nyunt, 'Speech on the Developments and Progressive Changes in Myanmar Naingngan', 30 August 2003; Khin Maung Win, 'Myanmar Roadmap to Democracy: The Way Forward', Presentation at the Seminar on Understanding Myanmar, Yangon, 27–8 January 2004.

56 Fabiola Desy Unidjaja, 'RI hopes to see Suu Kyi freed in October', *Jakarta Post*, 31 July 2003, p. 1.

57 'Burma warned over Suu Kyi', BBC News Online, 24 September 2003: http://news.bbc.co.uk/1/hi/world/asia-pacific/3134552.stm.

58 'Time for Rangoon to show its plans', *Bangkok Post*, 15 December 2003.

59 Participating countries included Australia, Austria, Italy, Germany, France, China, Japan, India, Singapore, Indonesia and Thailand. Ambassador Razali Ismail was also present. See Thet Khaing, 'Govt praises Thai initiative in hosting Bangkok forum', *Myanmar Times*, December 22–8, 2003.

60 Rungrawee C. Pinyorat, 'Junta to release Suu Kyi', *The Nation*, 4 April 2004: http://www.yuyu.net/burmanet2-l/archive/0332.html.

61 For a fuller discussion see Haacke, '"Enhanced Interaction" with Myanmar

and the Project of a Security Community', pp. 199–200.

[62] In this incident of 25 October 2004, following mass protests in connection with arrests in Tak Bai of local men suspected of providing weapons to insurgents operating in southern Thailand, 78 people suffocated when hundreds of mostly young Muslims were transported to an army camp for detention.

[63] Statement by the ASEAN Foreign Ministers, Vientiane, 25 July 2005: www. aseansec.org/17589.htm.

[64] Personal communication, May 2005.

[65] Transcript of Yeo's Media Conference on Myanmar's Chairmanship of ASEAN, 38th AMM, 26 July 2005.

[66] *Threat to the Peace: A Call for the UN Security Council to Act in Burma*, A Report commissioned by The Honorable Vàclav Havel and Bishop Desmond M. Tutu, prepared by DLA Piper Rudnick Gray Cary, 20 September 2005: http:// www.burmacampaign.org.uk/reports/ Burmaunscreport.pdf.

[67] See AIPMC Press Statement: 'Time for the Security Council to discuss Myanmar', 23 September 2005: http://www.aseanmp. org/index.php?option=com_content&tas k=blogcategory&id=5&Itemid=20.

[68] 'Myanmar democracy will not lead to chaos-envoy', *Reuters*, 12 October 2005.

[69] Clive Parker, 'Philippines to Support UN Action on Burma', *The Irrawaddy*, 22 November 2005; see also 'PGMA: RP to join UN efforts to speed up democratic reforms in Myanmar', 19 November 2005: http://www.macapagal.com/gma/act.html.

[70] Security Council Report, Update Report, Myanmar, 15 December 2004, no. 4: http://www.securitycouncilreport.org/ site/c.glKWLeMTIsG/b.1304015/k.247A/ UPDATE_REPORT_NO_4brMYAN-MARBR15_DECEMBER_2005.htm.

[71] Chairman's Statement of the 11th ASEAN Summit, 'One Vision, One Identity, One Community', Kuala Lumpur, 12 December 2005: http://www.aseansec.org/18039.htm.

[72] Jonathan Kent, 'Malaysia 'hopeful' on Burma move', *BBC News/Asia Pacific*, 11 December 2005, http://news.bbc.co.uk/2/ hi/asia-pacific/4519202.stm.

[73] Personal communication.

[74] 'Editorial: A Tactical Blunder', *The Irrawaddy*, vol. 14, no. 4, April 2006, p. 3.

[75] R. Ravichandran, 'M'sia Says Myanmar Need Not Be Referred To UN Security Council', *Bernama*, 20 January 2006: http://www.thebroker.com.my/bernama/ v3/news_lite.php?id=176574.

[76] Michael Vatikiotis, 'Indonesia back on the world stage', *Asia Times*, 30 March 2006:http://www.atimes.com/atimes/ Southeast_Asia/HC30Ae01.html.

Chapter Four

[1] In line with the development of the situation in Myanmar and the refinement of policy in Washington, repeated adjustments have been made to the language in which US foreign policy objectives towards Myanmar have been couched; see the semi-annual Reports to Congress on the Conditions in Burma and US Policy Toward Burma, for the period 2001–2005 at: http://www.state. gov/p/eap/rls/rpt/burma/; for the period 1996–2000 see http://www.state.gov/www/ regions/eap/us-burma_report.html.

[2] For US activities to support democracy in Myanmar, see US Department of State,

'Report on activities to support democracy activists in Burma as required by the Burmese Freedom and Democracy Act of 2003', 30 October 2003: http://www.state. gov/p/eap/rls/rpt/burma/26017.htm.

[3] The Generalised System of Tariff Preferences was recommended by the United Nations Conference on Trade and Development in 1968. Under this scheme industrialised countries would grant trade preferences to all developing countries. The European Community first implemented its GSP scheme in 1971.

4   For details on Japan's temporary 'freeze' of ODA see Yuki Akimoto, 'A Yen to Help the Junta', *The Irrawaddy*, vol. 12, no. 10, October 2004, p. 18.

5   Toshihiro Kudo, 'The Impact of the United States Sanctions on the Myanmar Garment Industry', Discussion Paper no. 42, (Chiba: Institute of Developing Economies, Japan External Trade Organisation, December 2005): http://www.ide.go.jp/English/Publish/Dp/pdf/042_kudo.pdf.

6   Bureau of East Asian and Pacific Affairs, US Department of State, 'Conditions in Burma and US Policy Toward Burma for the Period March28, 2004–September 27, 2004': www.state.gov/p/eap/rls/rpt/36721.htm.

7   'Interview with Colonel Hla Min' by *Channel-J News Agency*, printed in Hla Min, *Political Situation of the Union of Myanmar and its Role in the Region* (Yangon: Ministry of Defence, 2004), p. 151.

8   This draws on Selth, 'Burma's Muslims and the War on Terror', *Studies in Conflict & Terrorism*, vol. 27, no. 2, March–April 2004, p. 117.

9   Bureau of East Asian and Pacific Affairs, US Department of State, 'Conditions in Burma and US Policy Toward Burma for the Period September 28, 2003–March 27, 2004': www.state.gov/p/eap/rls/rpt/31335.htm.

10 See Ardeth Maung Thawnghmung, 'Preconditions and Prospects for Democratic Transition in Burma/Myanmar', *Asian Survey*, vol. 43, no. 3, May/June 2003, p. 453.

11 Bureau of East Asian and Pacific Affairs, US Department of State, 'Conditions in Burma and US Policy Toward Burma for the Period March 28, 2002–September 27, 2002': www.state.gov/p/eap/rls/rpt/burma/19283.htm.

12 Steinberg, 'Myanmar: Reconciliation-Progress in the Process?', *Southeast Asian Affairs 2003*, pp. 173–4.

13 Bureau of East Asian and Pacific Affairs, US Department of State, 'Conditions in Burma and US Policy Toward Burma for the Period, September 28, 2002–March 27, 2003': www.state.gov/p/eap/rls/rpt/burma/19554.htm.

14 Powell, 'It's Time to Turn the Tables on Burma's Thugs', originally published in the *Wall Street Journal*, 12 June 2003: http://www.state.gov/secretary/former/powell/remarks/2003/21466.htm.

15 Hla Min, *Political Situation of the Union of Myanmar and Its Role in the Region*, p. 16.

16 'Burmese Woo Congressional Aides', *Far Eastern Economic Review*, 12 December 2002, p. 10. The contract, it is argued, was not extended due to the failure to win certification on narcotics cooperation. Myanmar also does not have the resources required for a long and intensive lobbying campaign on the hill.

17 Matthew P. Daley, Deputy Assistant Secretary, Bureau of East Asian and Pacific Affairs, US Department of State, 'Response to Question submitted for the record by Dana Rohrbacher', in 'Developments in Burma', Joint Hearing before the Subcommittee on Asia and the Pacific and the Subcommittee on International Terrorism, Nonproliferation and Human Rights of the Committee on International Relations, House of Representatives, 108th Session, 25 March 2004, p. 99.

18 Steinberg, 'Burma/Myanmar: A Guide for the Perplexed?', in Badgley, ed., 'Reconciling Burma/Myanmar: Essays on US Relations with Burma', pp. 50–1.

19 'Unimpressed By Burma's War on Drugs', *Far Eastern Economic Review*, 5 December 2002, p. 10.

20 McConnell, 'Sanctions are the most effective weapon against Burma's military regime', *Time Asia*, 23 January 2006: http://www.time.com/time/asia/covers/501060130/burma_vpt.html. Senators McConnell, Richard Lugar and Dianne Feinstein as well as Congressman Tom Lantos participated in the *Burma: Time for Change*, Report of an Independent Task Force, sponsored by the Council on Foreign Relations, 2003. For their additional views see pp. 34–6 of the report: http://www.cfr.org/publication/6054/burma.html.

21 US Department of State, 'Conditions in Burma and US Policy Toward Burma for the Period March 28, 2004–September 27, 2004'.

22 *Ibid.*

23 Thet Khaing, 'US report riddled with errors: Govt', *Myanmar Times*, vol. 11, no. 207, 8–14 March 2004.

24 'Aung San Suu Kyi not on hunger strike, Thai FM', *People's Daily Online*, 5 September 2003: http:English.people.com.cn/200309/05/eng20030905_123761.shtml; 'U.S.criticizes Suu Kyi treatment', CNN.com, 7 September 2003.

25 Thet Khaing with *Agence France-Presse*, 'Sanctions and isolation are a 'lose-lose' strategy for all, USA must adopt fresh approach: Govt', *Myanmar Times*, vol. 10, no. 189, 27 October–2 November 2003.

26 'Myanmar: Versuchs-Kernreaktor, *Südostasien aktuell*, July 2001, p. 362.

27 Selth, *Burma's North Korean Gambit: A Challenge to Regional Security?*, Canberra Papers on Strategy and Defence, no.154 (Canberra: Strategic and Defence Studies Centre, Australian National University, 2004), p. 27.

28 Lintner and Shawn W. Crispin, 'Dangerous Bedfellows', *Far Eastern Economic Review*, 20 November 2003, p. 22–4.

29 'Concern Over Burma–North Korea Ties', *Far Eastern Economic Review*, 16 October 2003, p. 14.

30 'Myanmar-North Korea Nuclear, Missile Cooperation Alleged', *Asian Export Control Observer*, no. 1, April 2004, p. 11: http://cns.miis.edu/pubs/observer/asian/pdfs/aeco_0404.pdf; Keith Luse, the aide in question, raised the point again in a speech at the Heritage Foundation on 9 April 2004. See Paul Kerr, 'US accuses Burma of seeking weapons technology', *Arms Control Today*, May 2004;www.armscontrol.org/act/2004_05/Burma.asp.

31 Quoted in 'Burma denies Korea Nuclear Link', *Far Eastern Economic Review*, 11 March 2004, p. 9.

32 Quoted in 'North Korean Nukes in Burma', *Far Eastern Economic Review*, 15 April 2004, p. 10.

33 Daley, Prepared Statement before the House Committee on International Relations, Subcommittee on East Asia and the Pacific and the Subcommittee on International Terrorism, Non-proliferation and Human Rights, House of Representatives, 108th Session, Washington DC, 25 March 2004: http://wwwc.house.gov/international_relations/108/dale032504.htm.

34 Myanmar has signed and/or ratified the 1963 Partial Test Ban Treaty, the 1967 Outer Space Treaty, the 1968 Nuclear Non-Proliferation Treaty; it signed the 1972 Seabed Treaty and the 1995 Treaty on the Southeast Asia Nuclear Weapons Free Zone. See Selth, Burma's Armed Forces, chapter 10 ('Burma and Exotic Weapons').

35 Selth, *Burma's North Korean Gambit*, p. 34.

36 Personal Communication, August 2005.

37 See Sergei Blagov, 'From Myanmar to Russia with love', *Asia Times*, 12 April 2006: http://www.atimes.com/atimes/Southeast_Asia/HD12Ae01.html.

38 'Myanmar agrees to restore ties with North Korea-sources', *Reuters*, 11 April 2006: http://asia.news.yahoo.com/060410/3/2iu5l.html.

39 The United States Security Strategy for the East Asia-Pacific Region 1998: http://www.defenselink.mil/pubs/easr98/.

40 Cohen, *DoD News Briefing*, 01 October 1999: http://www.defenselink.mil/transcripts/1999/t10011999_t001bang.html.

41 Aung Zaw, 'The Upturned Chair', *The Irrawaddy*, vol. 13, no. 8, August 2005 p. 17.

42 Paula J. Dobriansky, Under Secretary for Democracy and Global Affairs, US Department of State, 'Toward a Free and Democratic Burma', Remarks at Brookings-Bern Project on Internal Displacement with National Endowment for Democracy and Church World Service, Washington DC, 26 October 2005: http://www.state.gov/g/rls/rm/2005/55844.htm.

43 The US administration repeated the claims, but the military government rejected them unequivocally, admitting only to isolated cases of rape.

44 On the background, see 'US to Intensify Pressure on Burma', *The Irrawaddy*, vol. 14, no.1, January 2006, p. 8.

45 Briefing with US Trade Representative Rob Portman, Busan, South Korea, 16 November 2005: http://www.state.gov/secretary/rm/2005/56940.htm.

46 'President Discusses Freedom and Democracy in Kyoto, Japan', 16 November 2005: http://www.whitehouse.gov/news/releases/2005/11/20051116-6.html.

47 Hill, 'Asian Pariah', *Wall Street Journal*, 4 January 2006: http://www.burmanet.org/news/2006/01/04/wall-street-journal-asian-pariah-christopher-hill/.

48 Hill, 'Burma: Update and Next Steps', Statement before the House International Relations Committee, Washington DC, 7 February 2006: http://www.state.gov/p/eap/rls/rm/60553.htm; Eric G. John, 'Burma: Update and Next Steps', Statement before the Senate Foreign Relations Committee, Subcommittee on East Asia and the Pacific, Washington DC, 29 March 2006: www.state.gov/p/eap/rls/rm/63839.htm.

49 Hill, 'East Asia in Transition: Opportunities and Challenges for the United States', Statement to the Asia and the Pacific Subcommittee of the House International Relations Committee, Washington DC, 8 March 2006, http://www.state.gov/p/eap/rls/rm/62755.htm.

50 Cited in 'Myanmar's Military is "Impervious" to Criticism, Kelly Says', *Bloomberg*, 3 June 2004.

51 'Junta Hits Back at US', *The Irrawaddy*, 24 May 2004.

52 Samuel Blythe, 'Myanmar's junta fears US invasion', *Asia Times*, 28 April 2006.

53 Lintner and Crispin, 'Dangerous Bedfellows', p. 24.

54 For this and other explanations see Aung Zaw, 'Dreams of a Rat Hole', *The Irrawaddy*, vol. 13, no. 4, April 2005, pp. 8–10; 'Retreat to the Jungle', *The Irrawaddy*, vol. 13, no. 12, December 2005, pp. 28–9.

55 Burma UN Service Office, National Coalition Government of the Union of Burma and The Burma Fund, *The Crisis in Burma: An Agenda for the United Nations Security Council?* (Washington DC: The Burma Fund, October 2003): http://www.kus.uu.se/Burma/Burma_UNSC.pdf.

56 A comprehensive analysis can be found in Steinberg, *Burma: The State of Myanmar* (Washington DC: Georgetown University Press, 2001), chapter 9.

57 Guyot, 'Myanmar: Several Endings, No Clear Beginnings', in Daljit Singh and Liak Teng Kiat, eds, *Southeast Asian Affairs 1996* (Singapore: ISEAS, 1996), p. 265; personal communication, August 2005.

58 Japanese Ministry of Foreign Affairs, Statement by the Minister for Foreign Affairs of Japan on the Lifting of the House Arrest of Daw Aung San Suu Kyi, 11 July 1995: http://www.mofa.go.jp/announce/announce/archive_2/suukyi.html.

59 Steinberg, *Burma: The State of Myanmar*, p. 258.

60 Patrick Köllner, 'Japan's Engagement in Myanmar: Zwischen Demokratieförderung und Geschäftsinteressen', *Südostasien aktuell*, January 1999, pp. 64–71.

61 Japanese Ministry of Foreign Affairs, 'Japan-Myanmar Relations': http://www.mofa.go.jp/region/asia-paci/myanmar/index.html.

62 Japanese Ministry of Foreign Affairs, 'Yoriko Kawaguchi's Visit to Myanmar (Overview and Evaluation)', 6 August 2002: http://www.mofa.go.jp/region/asia-paci/asean/fmv0207/myanmar.html.

63 Burma Information Network-Japan, 'Is Japan really getting tough on Burma? (Not likely)', 28 June 2003: http://www.ibiblio.org/obl/docs/bi_on_oda.htm.

64 For an overview of Japan's ODA to mostly non-governmental recipients in Myanmar see Yuki Akimoto, 'A Yen to help the junta', *The Irrawaddy*, vol. 12, no. 10, October 2004, p. 18.

65 See Karen E. Smith, 'The EU, human rights and relations with third countries: "foreign policy" with an ethical dimension?', in Smith and Margot Light, eds, *Ethics and Foreign Policy* (Cambridge: Cambridge University Press, 2001), pp. 185–203.

66 European Commission, 'The EU's Relations with Burma/Myanmar': http://europa.eu.int/comm/external_relations/myanmar/intro/; European Commission, DG Trade, EU Bilateral Trade and Trade with the World: Myanmar, 9 March 2006.

67 Personal communication, Yangon, August 2005.

68 European Commission, 'Burma/Myanmar - Council Conclusions: General Affairs Council,9 April 2001: http://ec.europa.eu/comm/external_relations/human_rights/doc/gac_conclbm.htm.

69 European Union, Council Common Position (2001/757/CFSP) of 29 October 2001, extending and amending Common Position 96/635/CFSP on Burma/Myanmar, in Official Journal of the European Communities L 286/1, 30 October 2001.

70 European Union, Council Common Position of 21 October 2002 amending and extending Common Position 96/635/CFSP on Burma/Myanmar, in Official Journal of the European Communities L285, vol. 45, 23 October 2002.

71 European Union, General Affairs and External Relations Council, 'Burma/Myanmar-Council Conclusions', 14 April 2003.

72 European Union, Council Common Position of 21 October 2002.

73 Council Conclusions, 16 June 2003: Burma/Myanmar, http://europa.eu.int/comm/external_relations/myanmar/intro/gac.htm#bu160603.

74 European Commission, 'Commissioner Ferrero-Waldner in Kyoto for the ASEM Foreign Ministers Meeting, 6–7 May 2005', 03 May 2005: http://europa.eu.int/comm/external_relations/news/ferrero/2005/sp05_534.htm.

75 European Commission, Humanitarian Aid Office, ECHO Decisions 2005: http://europa.eu.int/comm/echo/information/decisions/2005_en.cfm.

76 UK Department for International Development, Country Profiles, 'Burma': http://www.dfid.gov.uk/countries/asia/burma.asp.

77 For Total's overview of its activities in Myanmar, see 'Total in Myanmar: a sustained commitment': http://burma.total.com/en/publications/sustained_commitment.pdf.

78 Jörn Dosch, The Changing Dynamics of Southeast Asian Politics (Boulder, CO: Lynne Rienner, forthcoming), chapter 6.

79 Among the European institutions, the European Parliament has been the SPDC's sharpest critic.

80 Shada Islam, 'Europe plans more engagement in Burma', The Irrawaddy, vol. 13, no. 4, April 2005, pp. 15–16.

81 Hervé Jouanjean, Deputy Director General, External Relations, European Commission, 'National Reconciliation and Foreign Assistance – The Future of the People is Our Challenge', Burma/Myanmar Day, Brussels, 5 April 2005: http://www.ibiblio.org/obl/docs3/Burma_Day_KeyNote_Speech.htm; Taylor and Morten Pedersen, 'Supporting Burma/Myanmar's national reconciliation process: challenges and opportunities. An independent report for the European Commission', January 2005: http://www.ibiblio.org/obl/docs3/Independant_Report-Burma_Day.htm.

82 '2006 State of the Union Address', Washington DC, 31 January 2006: http://www.state.gov/r/pa/ei/wh/rem/60153.htm.

Chapter Five

1   Liang, *Burma's Foreign Relations: Neutralism in Theory and Practice*, (Boulder, CO: Praeger, 1990), pp. 59–60, 197.

2   For the biography of U Thant see: http://www.un.org/Overview/SG/sg3bio.html.

3   This chapter does not address Myanmar's problems with the ILO. For an overview of the issues at hand see Jim Andrews, 'Showdown Time: ILO Sanctions loom as Burma spits defiance', *The Irrawaddy*, vol. 13, no. 3, March 2005, pp. 16–19.

4   A number of UN organisations operate in Myanmar, including the United Nations Development Programme, the United Nations Children's Fund, the Food and Agriculture Organisation of the United Nations, the World Health Organisation, UNHCR, the Joint United Nations Programme on HIV/AIDS, the World Food Programme and the United Nations Office on Drugs and Crime.

5   UNGA, 59th Session, Resolution Adopted by the General Assembly, 59/263. Situation of human rights in Myanmar, A/RES/59/263, 23 December 2004.

6   United Nations, Economic and Social Council, Commission on Human Rights, 61st Session, Summary Record of the 50th Meeting, 14 April 2005, E/CN.4/2005/SR.50, 21 April 2005.

7   Compare UNGA, Situation of human rights in Myanmar, A/Res/59/263, 23 December 2004 and UNGA, Situation in Myanmar, A/RES/46/132, 17 December 1991.

8   Derek Tonkin, 'A Critical Analysis of Havel–Tutu Report on Myanmar/Burma', Free Burma Coalition, 4 October 2005: http://www.freeburmacoalition.org/derektonkinonhaveltutureport.htm.

9   UNGA, Situation of Human Rights in Myanmar, 18 November 2005, A/C/3/60/L/53-Motion (Cuba): http://www.un.org/ga/60/third/i71cl53motion.pdf.

10 UNCHR, Situation of human rights in Myanmar, Commission on Human Rights Resolution 1992/58, 3 March 1992, E/CN.4/RES/1992/58.

11 UNGA, Letter from the Permanent Representative of Myanmar to the United Nations addressed to the UNSG, 11 November 1997, A/C.3/52/5.

12 UNGA, 51st Session, Situation of human rights in Myanmar, Note by the Secretary-General, General Assembly, A/51/466, 8 October 1996.

13 UNGA, 51st Session, Letter dated 13 December 1996 from the Permanent Representative of Myanmar to the United Nations addressed to the President of the UNGA, 16 December 1996, A/51/738.

14 The military government has been reluctant to allow for visits to Shan State, in part owing to the security situation on the ground.

15 United Nations, Economic and Social Council, Commission on Human Rights, 58th Session, Note verbale dated 27 March 2002 from the Permanent Mission of Myanmar to the United Nations Office at Geneva, E/CN.4/2002.158.

16 United Nations, Economic and Social Council, Commission on Human Rights, 59th Session, Note verbale dated 18 March 2003 from the Permanent Mission of Myanmar to the United Nations Office at Geneva, E/CN.4/2003/G/47, 21 March 2003, p. 3.

17 UNCHR, Interim Report of the Special Rapporteur of the Commission on Human Rights on the Situation of Human Rights in Myanmar, A/58/219, 5 August 2003.

18 United Nations Economic and Social Council, Commission on Human Rights, 60th Session, Situation of human rights in Myanmar, Report submitted by the Special Rapporteur, 5 January 2004, E/CN.4/2004/33.

19 *Ibid.*, p. 12.

20 'UN envoy slams Myanmar assembly', *Taipei Times*, 2 June 2004: http://www.taipeitimes.com/News/world/archives/2004/06/02/2003157928.

21 United Nations Economic and Social Council, 61st Session, Situation of human rights in Myanmar, Report of the Special

Rapporteur Paulo Sérgio Pinheiro, E/CN.4/2005/36, 2 December 2004.

22 UNGA, 60th Session, Interim report of the Special Rapporteur of the Commisson on Human Rights on the situation of human rights in Myanmar, A/60.221, 12 August 2005.

23 United Nations, Economic and Social Council, Report of the Special Rapporteur on the situation of human rights in Myanmar, E/CN.4/2006/34, 7 February 2006, p. 3.

24 Ibid.

25 The Human Rights Council was established in March 2006. It will convene for the first time on 19 June 2006. On its remit and powers, see: UNGA, Resolution 60/251 Human Rights Council, 15 March 2006, A/RES/60/251.

26 UNGA, 49th Session, Situation of human rights in Myanmar, Report of the Secretary-General, General Assembly A/49/716, 25 November 1994.

27 United Nations, General Assembly, 50th Session, Situation of human rights in Myanmar, Report of the Secretary-General, A/50/782, 24 November 1995.

28 United Nations Economic and Social Council, Commission on Human Rights, 57th Session, Report of the Secretary-General on the situation of human rights in Myamar, 22 March 2001, E/CN.4/2001/33.

29 UNGA, 56th session, Situation of human rights in Myanmar, Report of the Secretary-General, 24 October 2001, A/56/505.

30 United Nations Economic and Social Council, Commission on Human Rights, 59th Session, Situation of Human Rights in Myanmar, Report of the Secretary-General submitted pursuant to General Assembly resolution 57/231, 10 March 2003, E/CN.4/2003/33.

31 'UN envoy's mission makes no headway', Bangkok Post, 4 October 2003.

32 United Nations, Economic and Social Council, 60th Session, Report of the Secretary-General, Situation of human rights in Myanmar, 3 March 2004, E/CN.4/2004/30.

33 One example is the meeting between Nyan Win and the special envoy on the occasion of the ASEAN Summit in Vientiane in November 2004.

34 In part, these suspicions have fed on the previous and subsequent work-related links of one of Razali's assistants.

35 Personal communication. See also 'An Interview with Razali Ismail: Thoughts of Former UN Envoy', The Irrawaddy, 10 January 2006: http://www.irrawaddy.org/aviewer.asp?a=5348&z=6.

36 Burma UN Service Office, National Coalition Government of the Union of Burma and The Burma Fund, The Crisis in Burma.

37 United Nations, Economic and Social Council, Commission on Human Rights, Sixty-first session, Report of the Secretary-General on the situation of human rights in Myanmar, 7 March 2005, E/CN.4/2005/130.

38 UNGA, Situation on human rights in Myanmar, Report by the Secretary-General, 10 October 2005, A/60/422.

39 'An Interview with Razali Ismail: Thoughts of Former UN Envoy'.

40 For an apparent exception see Dana R. Dillon, 'Time for a U.N. Security Council Resolution on Burma', Executive Memorandum no. 990, The Heritage Foundation: http://www.heritage.org/Research/AsiaandthePacific/em990.cfm.

41 DLA Piper Rudnick Gray Cary on behalf on Havel and Tutu, Threat to the Peace, p. 59. For a counterpoint to several issues contained in the report see Tonkin, 'A Critical Analysis of Havel–Tutu Report on Myanmar/Burma'.

42 United Nations, Commission on Human Rights, 62nd Session, The situation of human rights in Myanmar, Report of the Secretary-General, 27 February 2006, E/CN.4/2006/117. Emphasis added.

43 The Global Fund fights AIDS, Tuberculosis and Malaria. In August 2005 it announced its withdrawal from Myanmar by the end of the year because in light of new procedures for travel

clearances and the procurement of medical and other supplies, its grants to the UNDP could no longer be managed in a way that would have ensured effective programme implementation. The United States is by far the largest donor to the Global Fund.

44 United Nations, Commission on Human Rights, 62nd Session, The situation of human rights in Myanmar, Report of the Secretary-General, 27 February 2006, E/CN.4/2006/117, p. 4.

45 UNSG, 'Under-Secretary-General Gambari to Visit Myanmar, Beginning 19 May', 16 May 2006: http://www.un.org/News/Press/docs/2006/sgsm10464.doc.htm.

46 Situations in which a 'pocket veto' is used are those in which a procedural matter is open to simple majority vote, but where permanent members rely on the threat of their veto power to prevent a matter from being placed formally on the UNSC agenda. The 'pocket veto' is also known as the 'hidden veto'.

Conclusion

1 Steinberg, 'Myanmar: Reconciliation-Progress in the Process?'

2 United Nations, Economic and Social Council, Situation of Human Rights in Myanmar, Report of the Special Rapporteur, 7 February 2006, p. 8.

3 'Bomb blasts in Burma – A Chronology', The Irrawaddy: http://www.irrawaddy.org/aviewer.asp?a=5762&z=14.

4 Martin T. Smith, 'Ethnic Politics and Regional Development in Myanmar: The Need for New Approaches', in Myanmar: Beyond Politics to Societal Imperatives, pp. 72–3.

5 See Aung Zaw, 'The Politics of Peace', The Irrawaddy, November 2005, pp. 8–9; Aung Lwin Oo, 'Junta urges the Wa's Army to Disarm', The Irrawaddy, 18 April 2006.

6 This includes the Kachin Independence Organisation, the New Mon State Party and Karen Democratic Buddhist Army; Shah Paung, 'Ceasefire groups defiant', The Irrawaddy, 14 October 2005. Major elements of the SSA-North are also unwilling to disarm.

7 Khun Sam, 'KIO hold emergency meeting', The Irrawaddy, 12 April 2006; Louis Reh, 'Burmese junta cuts support for NMSP', The Irrawaddy, 9 September 2005.

8 In protest, the New Mon State Party boycotted the NC session in December 2005, sending only observers.

9 Six legal ethnic-minority parties participated in the NC in 2005: Kokang Democracy and Unity Party, Union Kayin League, Union Pa-O National Organisation, Mro or Khami National Solidarity Organisation, Lahu National Development Party and Wa National Development Party. The two parties not participating are the Shan Nationalities League for Democracy and the Shan State Kokang Democracy Party.

10 See contributions in Badgley, ed., 'Reconciling Burma/Myanmar: Essays on U.S. Relations with Burma'. Not changing the structure of sanctions despite Myanmar's genuine efforts to build a common platform for change is also seen as having undermined reformers within the Myanmar military who were inclined to seek a compromise with ASSK, as well as having strengthened sentiments of defiance among the leadership.

11 Ian Holliday, 'Rethinking the United States's Myanmar Policy', Asian Survey, vol. 45, no. 4, 2005, p. 618.

12 ICG, 'Myanmar: Sanctions, Engagement or Another Way Forward?', ICG Asia Report no. 78, 26 April 2004, p. iii: http://www.crisisgroup.org/home/index.cfm?id=2677&l=1.

13 Donald M. Seekins, 'Burma and U.S. Sanctions: Punishing an Authoritarian Regime', Asian Survey, vol. 45, no. 3, 2005, p. 450.

14 Neil A. Englehart, 'Is Regime Change enough for Burma? The Problem of State

Capacity', *Asian Survey*, vol. 45, no. 4, 2005, pp. 640–44.

15 See the contributions in Kyaw Yin Hlaing, Taylor and Tin Maung Maung Than, eds, *Myanmar: Beyond Politics to Societal Imperatives*.

16 ICG, *Myanmar: Sanctions, Engagement or Another Way Forward?*, pp. 28–36.

17 Pedersen, 'The Challenges of Transition in Myanmar', in Kyaw Yin Hlaing, Taylor and Tin Maung Maung Than, eds, *Myanmar: Beyond Politics to Societal Imperatives*, pp. 161–83.

18 Pedersen, 'The Crisis in Burma/ Myanmar: Foreign Aid as a Tool for Democratization', in Badgley, ed., 'Reconciling Burma/Myanmar: Essays on U.S. Relations with Burma', *NBR Analysis*, pp. 98–101.

19 Ashley South, 'Political Transition in Myanmar: A New Model for Democratization', *Contemporary Southeast Asia*, vol. 26, no. 2, August 2004, p. 251.

20 ICG, *Myanmar: Aid to the Border Areas*, ICG Asia Report, no. 82, 9 September 2004. For a critical view see David Scott Mathieson, 'The ICG, Burma, and the Politics of Diversion', *The Irrawaddy*, October 2004, pp. 25–6.

21 Zarni and May Oo, Free Burma Coalition, *Common Problems, Shared Responsibilities: Citizens' Quest for National Reconciliation in Burma/Myanmar*.

22 Eneko Landaburu, European Commission External Relations Directorate General, 'Supporting People – Assisting Transition', Burma/Myanmar Forum, Brussels, 29 March 2006: http://www.eias.org/conferences/2006/burma290306/landaburu.pdf.

23 'How to save it: Ostracising Myanmar has not helped its people. It is time to explore the possibility of a deal', *Economist*, 21 July 2005.

24 US assistance to groups of people inside Myanmar focuses on combating HIV/ AIDS and other infectious diseases (US$2m). See John, 'Burma: Update and Next Steps', 29 March 2006, www. http://www.state.gov/p/eap/rls/rm/63839.htm.

25 Senate Resolution 484, 18 May 2006.

26 Zarni and May Oo, Free Burma Coalition, *Common Problems, Shared Responsibilities: Citizens' Quest for National Reconciliation in Burma/Myanmar*, pp. 40–41.

27 *Ibid.*, pp. 11, 16, 17, 22. Interestingly, when Australia proposed in 1999 to try to negotiate with Myanmar on the establishment of an independent human rights institution (in line with the Indonesian example) this provoked a fierce response from ASSK who rejected the idea as 'ill advised'. See Tom Wingfield, 'Myanmar: Political Stasis and a Precarious Economy', in Daljit Singh, ed., *Southeast Asian Affairs 2000* (Singapore: ISEAS, 2000), pp. 210–11.

28 See Nandar Chann, 'Opposition Blues', *The Irrawaddy*, February 2005, pp. 16–17 and Kyaw Yin Hlaing, 'Myanmar in 2004: Why Military Rule Continues', in *Southeast Asian Affairs 2005*, especially pp. 238–44.

29 See Responses from Daley, Deputy Assistant Secretary, to Questions Submitted for the Record by The Honorable James A. Leach, Chairman of Subcommittee on Asia and the Pacific, Developments in Burma: Joint Hearing before the Subcommittee on Asia and the Pacific and the Subcommittee on International Terrorism, Nonproliferation and Human Rights, 25 March 2004, Serial No. 108–23, p. 97: http://wwwa. house.gov/international_relations/108/ dale032504.htm.

30 See for example Taylor, 'The Outlook for Myanmar and its Role in the Region'.

31 See Maung Cedana, 'Wearing the same old nether garment', pp. 8–9.

32 See the separate written statements submitted by Steinberg and Pedersen, *Developments in Burma*, Joint Hearing before the Subcommittee on Asia and the Pacific and the Subcommittee on International Terrorism, Nonproliferation and Human Rights, 25 March 2004, Serial No. 108–23, p. 60 and p. 67: http://wwwa. house.gov/international_relations/108/ steio32504.htm; http://wwwa.house.gov/ international_relations/108/pede032504. htm.

[33] See also Steinberg, 'Burma: Who's Isolating Whom?', *Far Eastern Economic Review*, 11 March 2004, p. 22. Also see his 'Burma/Myanmar: A Guide for the Perplexed?' in Badgley, ed., 'Reconciling Burma/Myanmar: Essays on U.S. Relations with Burma', *NBR Analysis*, pp. 41–54.